MC

D0983350

WITHDRAWN

HEGEL TODAY

Hegel Today

Edited by
BERNARD CULLEN
Department of Scholastic Philosophy
The Queen's University of Belfast

Avebury

Aldershot · Brookfield USA · Hong Kong · Singapore · Sydney

Published by
Avebury
Gower Publishing Company Limited,
Gower House, Croft Road, Aldershot, Hants GU11 3HR,
England

Gower Publishing Company,
Old Post Road, Brookfield, Vermont 05036,
United States of America.

British Library Cataloguing in Publication Data

Hegel today.
  1. Hegel, Georg Wilhelm Friedrich
  I. Cullen, Bernard
  193   B2948

Library of Congress Cataloging-in-Publication Data

Hegel today.

  Includes bibliographies.
  1. Hegel, Georg Wilhelm Friedrich, 1770-1831.
I. Cullen, Bernard.
B2948.H345 1988   193   87-27538
ISBN 0-566-05353-5

Printed and bound in Great Britain by Athanaeum Press Ltd, Newcastle-upon-Tyne

Contents

Editor's Foreword

The present volume contains a collection of essays that illustrate something of the range of contemporary interest in the philosophy of G.W.F. Hegel. Five of them (those by Lamb, Cullen, Vincent, Hunt, and Pattman) deal with various aspects of Hegel's social and political philosophy, thereby reflecting accurately the dominant interest in Hegel studies today. A recurring theme in them, either centrally or incidentally, is the relation of Hegel to his most celebrated disciple, Karl Marx. Peter Hodgson's essay analyses the evolution of Hegel's attitude to Judaism; while Wolfgang Neuser examines an aspect of Hegel's philosophy of science that throws light on his mature dialectical method.

David Lamb's article is an expanded version of 'Teleology: Kant and Hegel', which first appeared in *Hegel's Critique of Kant,* edited by Stephen Priest, Clarendon Press, Oxford, 1987, and is published here with due acknowledgements to Stephen Priest and to the Clarendon Press. The articles by Geoffrey Hunt and Wolfgang Neuser first appeared in *Explorations in Knowledge,* vol. 3, no. 1 (1986), and are reprinted here with acknowledgements and thanks to that journal's editors. Peter C. Hodgson's article first appeared in *The Owl of Minerva,* vol. 19, no. 1 (1987), and is reprinted here with the permission of the editor, for which I am very grateful. The other three articles have been specially written for this volume and are published here for the first time.

I am very grateful to Dave Lamb, who first suggested the project. I owe a special debt of gratitude to the Vice-Chancellor of The Queen's University of Belfast, Dr Gordon Beveridge, for granting me access to the full facilities of this university's Secretarial Centre; and my heartfelt thanks go to Mrs Angela White (Supervisor of the Centre) and her staff, especially Mrs Lorna Goldstrom, Mrs Leslie Steer, and Miss Margaret Drumm, for their superb proficiency, their remarkable patience, and their unfailing good humour, without which this book could not have been prepared for printing.

Belfast, June 1987   Bernard Cullen

Contributors

David Lamb is Senior Lecturer in Philosophy in the University of Manchester. Among his eight books, he is author of *Hegel: From Foundation to System* (1979) and *Language and Perception in Hegel and Wittgenstein* (1980), joint editor (with L. Stepelevich) of *Hegel's Philosophy of Action* (1983), and editor of *Hegel and Modern Philosophy* (1987). He was the Secretary/Treasurer of the Hegel Society of Great Britain from 1979 to 1986.

Bernard Cullen, who lectures in the Department of Scholastic Philosophy in The Queen's University of Belfast, is author of *Hegel's Social and Political Thought* (1979). A Council member of the Hegel Society of Great Britain and Secretary of the National Committee for Philosophy of the Royal Irish Academy, he is founding Editor of the *Irish Philosophical Journal.* For the academic year 1987-88, he is a Research Fellow of the Alexander von Humboldt-Stiftung at the Hegel-Archiv in Bochum.

Andrew Vincent is Lecturer in Politics in University College, Cardiff. He is the author of *Theories of the State* and *Philosophy, Politics and Citizenship* (with R. Plant), editor of *The Philosophy of T.H. Green,* and joint editor (with M. George) of G.W.F. Hegel's *Philosophical Propaedeutic.*

Geoffrey Hunt is a post-doctoral Fellow in Philosophy at University College, Cardiff, having previously lectured at the National University of Lesotho and the University of Ife, Nigeria. His publications include articles in the *Journal of Applied Philosophy, The Philosophical Forum, Praxis International,* and *History of Political Thought.* He is currently completing a book on Gramsci and civil society.

Peter C. Hodgson is Professor of Theology in the Divinity School of Vanderbilt University, Nashville. He recently completed a new English edition of Hegel's *Lectures on the Philosophy of Religion,* and has written a number of books concerned with current issues in Christian theology.

Robert Pattman is Lecturer in Sociology at Queen Mary's College, Basingstoke. He has completed an MPhil degree at the University of Sheffield.

Wolfgang Neuser is a graduate in physics (theoretical astrophysics) and a PhD in philosophy, with a thesis on Hegel's philosophy of nature. His publications include a German translation, with introduction and commentary, of Hegel's *Dissertatio Philosophica de Orbitis Planetarum* (1986), and *Der Raum zwischen Logik und Erfahrung: Bemerkungen zu Hegels Naturphilosophie* (in press).

Abbreviations

DHE   *Dokumente zu Hegels Entwicklung,* ed. J. Hoffmeister, Frommann, Stuttgart, 1936.

HL   *Hegel's Logic. Being Part One of the Encyclopaedia of the Philosophical Sciences* [1830], trans. William Wallace, Clarendon Press, Oxford, third edition, 1975. (This is a reprint, with some minor corrections, of the translation previously published as *The Logic of Hegel.*)

HPM   *Hegel's Philosophy of Mind. Being Part Three of the Encyclopaedia of the Philosophical Sciences* [1830], trans. William Wallace and A.V. Miller, Clarendon Press, Oxford, 1971.

HPN   *Hegel's Philosophy of Nature. Being Part Two of the Encyclopaedia of the Philosophical Sciences* [1830], trans. A.V. Miller, Clarendon Press, Oxford, 1970.

HPR   *Hegel's Philosophy of Right,* trans. T.M. Knox, Clarendon Press, Oxford, 1952.

HSL   *Hegel's Science of Logic,* trans. W.H. Johnston and L.G. Struthers, Allen & Unwin, London, 1929.

LPR   *Lectures on the Philosophy of Religion,* 3 vols, ed. Peter C. Hodgson, trans. R.F. Brown, P.C. Hodgson, J.M. Stewart, University of California Press, Berkeley, Los Angeles, London, 1984-1987.

PH   *The Philosophy of History,* trans. J. Sibree, Dover Publications, New York, 1956.

PM   *The Phenomenology of Mind,* trans. J.B. Baillie, second edition, Allen & Unwin, London, 1949.

PS   *Phenomenology of Spirit,* trans. A.V. Miller, Clarendon Press, Oxford, 1977.

RH   *Reason in History,* trans. Robert S. Hartman, Bobbs-Merrill, Indianapolis, 1953.

SLM   *Hegel's Science of Logic,* trans. A.V. Miller, Allen & Unwin, London, 1969.

1 Teleology and Hegel's Dialectic of History

DAVID LAMB

> A spider constructs operations that resemble those of a weaver, and a bee puts to shame many an architect in the construction of her cells. But what distinguishes the worst architect from the best of bees is this, that the architect raises his structure in imagination before he erects it in reality. At the end of every labour process we get a result that already existed in the imagination of the labourer at its commencement. He not only effects a change of form in the material on which he works, but he also realizes a purpose of his own that gives the law to his *modus operandi,* and to which he must subordinate his will.
>
> Karl Marx[1]

I Introduction

According to Lenin and Georg Lukács, Hegel's account of teleology is one of the true precursors of historical materialism. The extent of Marx's intellectual debt to Hegel is, of course, a matter of fierce dispute amongst contemporary Marxists, but the chapter on teleology in Hegel's *Science of Logic* does bear a fundamental resemblance to some of Marx's mature reflections in *Capital.* Not only does Hegel dramatize the unity of form and content in a materialist dialectic; he also draws together the related concepts of labour and the historic process. What Hegel attempts is nothing less than a reconciliation of efficient and final causes, mechanism and teleology, materiality and values, theory and practice, man and nature. It is no accident that this task is but a few pages away from his attempt to portray the unity of truth and virtue, epistemology and ethics. For Hegel, the good is a practical concept, bound up with action and will. It is hardly surprising that the chapter corresponding to 'The Good' in *Hegel's Logic* has for its title, 'The Will'.

Teleology is about purposiveness. In so far as it is concerned with human purpose it will invoke an ethical dimension, but its essentially human nature was not fully realized until Hegel. Classical philosophy saw purpose in nature and asserted the authority of God to vouch for it. Reacting against the concept of divine purpose the mechanistic materialists of the seventeenth century emphasized material causality at the expense of teleology. The latter, they held, was subjective, primitive, and unscientific. 'A final cause', said Hobbes, 'has no place but in such things as have sense and will; and this also I shall prove hereafter to be an efficient cause'.[2] To this day it is widely held that maturity in science accompanies a rejection of teleology. Thus a rigid gap is presupposed between efficient and final causes, with the consequential striving to reduce teleology to mechanism.

Interest in the concept of teleology was revived by Kant and his contemporaries. Although there was a fundamental difference between Kant and Hegel's account of teleology, by airing the subject Kant raised the relevant problems for Hegel to develop. One of the merits which Hegel saw in Kant's work was his notion of an 'internal teleology' which he contrasted with the external teleologies of classical philosophy and theology, according to which the world and its inhabitants serve the purpose of 'an extra-mundane under-standing'; a theory 'favoured by piety so much that it seemed to be removed from the true investigation of nature'.[3] It should be clear that Hegel's rejection of the external teleology of classical philosophy also rules out an interpretation of Hegel's own position in which he allegedly posits an external cosmic spirit which manipulates human history.

In a very important sense Kant followed the position outlined by Hobbes and the mechanistic materialists, who saw no place for teleology in explanations of the phenomenal world. Purpose entered into Kant's reflections on human activity only in his moral philosophy, where the concept of internal teleology was introduced to advance the view that man is an end in himself and should not, under any circumstances, be used as a means for another end. Hegel praised this development but was critical of what he saw as an abstract formulation of the relationship between ends and means.[4] For whilst Kant had drawn attention to certain facts about human beings, which were ignored by the mechanistic materialists, and thus rescued human dignity from blind causality, his approach nevertheless reiterates their assumption of an unbridgeable gulf between causality and teleology. On the one hand Kant presented a natural world, purposeless and subject to blind causality. On the other hand he presented a moral agent, purposive, free, and responsible. Hegel was duly critical of Kant's phenomenal-noumenal distinction and the battery of dichotomies which surrounded it, and his excellence lies in his acceptance of what is important in Kant - the concept of internal teleology and the restoration of human dignity - and in his ability to go beyond Kant in his analysis of human labour.

The earliest account of his work on the subject is found in the Jena lectures of 1805-6. Since they illustrate the direction of Hegel's thought in his *Science of Logic*, they are worth quoting at length:

> In tools or in the cultivated, fertilized field I possess a **possibility, content,** as **something general.** For this reason tools, the means, are to be preferred to the end or purpose of desire, which is more individual; the tools comprehend all the individualities.
>
> But a tool does not yet have activity in itself. I must still work with it. I have interposed **cunning** between myself and the external objects, so as to spare myself and to shield my determinacy and let it wear itself out. The Ego remains the soul of the syllogism, in reference to it, to activity. However, I only spare myself in terms of quantity, since I still get blisters. Making myself into a thing is still unavoidable; the activity of the impulse is not yet in the thing. It is important also to make the tool generate its own activity, to make it self-activating. This should be achieved (a) by contriving it so that its line, its thread, its double edge or whatever, is used to reverse its direction, to turn it in upon itself. Its passivity must be turned into activity, into a cohesive movement. (b) In general nature's own activity, the elasticity of a watch-spring, water, wind, etc. are employed to do things that they would not have done if left to themselves, so that their blind action is made purposive, the opposite of itself: the rational behaviour of nature, **laws,** in its external existence. Nothing happens to **nature** itself; the **individual purposes of natural existence** become universal. Here impulse departs entirely from labour. It allows nature to act on itself, simply looks on and controls it with a light touch: **cunning.** The broadside of force is assailed by the fine point of cunning. The *point d'honneur* of cunning in its struggle with force is to seize it on its blind side so that it is directed against itself, to take a firm grip on it, to be active against it or to turn it as movement back on itself, so that it annuls itself....[5]

Hegel's point here is simple to grasp. The teleology-mechanism dichotomy can be transcended by locating conscious human purpose **within** the causal network, without destroying it, or going beyond it. Hegel's insight is echoed in Marx's location of purpose within material causality:

> Labour is, in the first place, a process in which both man and Nature participate, and in which man of his own accord starts, regulates, and controls the material re-actions between himself and Nature. He opposes himself to Nature as one of her own forces, setting in motion arms and legs, head and hands, the natural forces of his body, in order to appropriate Nature's productions in a form adopted to his own wants. By thus acting on the external world and changing it, he at the same time changes his own nature.[6]

Despite numerous claims that Marx had completely divested himself of Hegelianism by the time he wrote *Capital,* the above remarks could easily have been written by Hegel. Both hold that whilst causal relationships are exploited to fulfil human purpose the latter is constantly modified and, indeed, transformed in the process. Hegel's treatment of teleology in his *Science of Logic* can be read as a detailed account of such a transformation. For Hegel, like Marx, the relationship between human needs and the instruments of labour is dialectical: the labour-process is rooted in human needs, and science and technology rest upon a social base which in turn engenders further causal relationships. In work one penetrates even deeper into the causal processes of the natural world. The limits of human knowledge are not transcendentally drawn, but are the functions of the purposes human agents set for themselves in the work process. Whilst human labour can never go beyond the limits of causality new developments consist in discovering hitherto concealed causal relationships which are then introduced into the labour process. Hobbes was correct in his contention that final causes are conditioned by efficient causes, but a greater understanding of efficient causes may be generated by finality, and in turn extend the freedom and scope of human purposiveness. In this way Hegel depicts the labour process as a means of extending our understanding of the natural world and as a further extension of freedom from causal determinism. Engels was therefore fully aware that Hegel had solved the problem of the relationship between freedom and necessity when he wrote in *Anti-Dühring*:

> Hegel was the first to state correctly the relation between freedom and necessity. To him freedom is the appreciation of necessity. 'Necessity is **blind** only **in so far as it is not understood**'. Freedom does not consist in the dream of independence from natural laws, but in the knowledge of these laws, and in the possibility this gives of systematically making them work towards definite ends.... Freedom therefore consists in the control over ourselves and over external nature, a control founded on knowledge of natural necessity; it is therefore a product of historical development. The first men who separated themselves from the animal kingdom were in all essentials as unfree as the animals themselves, but each step forward in the field of

culture was a step towards freedom. On the threshold of human history stands the discovery that mechanical motion can be transformed into heat: the production of fire by friction; at the close of the development so far gone through stands the discovery that heat can be transformed into mechanical motion: the steam engine.[7]

The social dynamic of the labour process is dramatized in Hegel's master-servant dialectic in the *Phenomenology* where freedom for the slave is not merely freedom from the master but from what was considered the natural limit of freedom - the hardness of the physical world.

Hegel's point is this: human beings make nature work for their own ends. Yet through this intervention the existing causal nexus may give birth to new causal relationships. This is a simple step, but a very important one in that it marks an advance upon previous attempts to understand the relationship between human beings and nature.

II Logic and Teleology

In Hegel's *Science of Logic* the insights of the Jena period are presented in a more systematic form. But the discussion of teleology remains one of the most obscure passages in his work. How is one to approach it?[8] When reading Hegel one must, like a detective, search for clues, for Hegel does not leave the reader without any familiar objects. In fact he gives three: a watch, a house, and a plough. These three objects symbolize his intentions and are the clues by means of which the complex argument can be unravelled. The watch is important because time is necessary for human purpose, a conscious end accomplished within a specific time at a particular period in history. The house symbolizes the desire to make the world habitable, to be at home in the world, to be free. Finally, the plough, an instrument of labour, represents human destiny. It is the key to the dialectic of history, symbolic of the relationship between humans and nature.

But what has all this to do with logic? For many of Hegel's predecessors and contemporary positivists, logic is concerned with a formal system of *a priori* rules which constitute an external standard for the validation of language and thought. But, like Wittgenstein, Hegel maintained that language (and thought) contains its own rules. Wittgenstein's remark that 'the rules of logical syntax must go without saying, once we know how each individual sign signifies'[9] is reminiscent of Hegel's unity of form and content. Consider the similarity between Wittgenstein's rejection of formalistic rules of inference and Hegel's remarks on formal logic. In the *Tractatus,* Wittgenstein is critical of the Russell-Frege laws of inference:

> If p follows from q, I can make an inference from q to p, deduce p from q.
> The nature of the inference can be gathered only from the two propositions.
> They themselves are the only possible justification of the inference.
> 'Laws of inference', which are supposed to justify inferences, as in the works of Frege and Russell, have no sense, and would be superfluous. (§5.132)

Hegel is less cryptic than Wittgenstein, but he too rejects the belief that the laws of logic are externally related to the drawing of an inference.

> If any one, when awaking on a winter morning, hears the creaking of the carriages on the street, and is thus led to conclude that it has frozen hard in the night, he has gone through a syllogistic operation: an operation which is every day repeated under the greatest variety of conditions. The interest, therefore, ought at least not to be less in becoming expressly conscious of this daily action of our thinking selves, than confessedly belongs to the study of the functions of organic life, such as the processes of digestion, assimilation, respiration, or even the processes and structures of the nature around us. We do not, however, for a moment deny that a study of Logic is no more necessary to teach us how to draw correct conclusions, than a previous study of anatomy and physiology is required in order to digest or breathe.[10]

What is being claimed is that if we know how to make an inference in any particular case then a knowledge of more general laws of inference is, as it were, implicitly acquired also. A sufficient justification for the inference of a conclusion from a set of premises will depend upon an understanding of the material content of the proposition concerned. To insist on any further justification is not to be extra-cautious; it is to display a misunderstanding of the nature of argument. Thus conceived, logic does not provide a set of rules externally related to language and argument, but is something contained within language. To possess a working familiarity with language is to possess a working familiarity with the rules of logic.

But just as language is bound up with human action so too must logical inference be understood within a behavioural context. Says Wittgenstein:

> An inference is a transition to an assertion; and so also to the behaviour that corresponds to the assertion. 'I draw the consequences' not only in words, but also in action.
> Was I justified in drawing these consequences? What is **called** a justification here? - How is the word

'justification' used? Describe language games. From these you will also see the importance of being justified.[11]

In an important sense logic, for Hegel, is not only bound up with behaviour, but is a reflection of a mode of social life. To this extent the dialectic of history is not externally related to history but is an integral feature of the particular actions of individuals and their institutions. Hegel's concept of logic will therefore cover matters which are not normally considered relevant to logic. In recent years, Wittgenstein's attack on the distinction between logic and other forms of discourse has been noted, but little attention has been paid to his closeness to Hegel in this respect. In *On Certainty,* one of the central questions posed by Wittgenstein is whether 'there is no sharp boundary between propositions of logic and empirical propositions'.[12]

Like Wittgenstein in *On Certainty,* Hegel calls into question the analytic-synthetic distinction, maintaining that the boundary line between sense and nonsense is not formally determined but is relative to the material content of the propositions concerned. Thus in his notorious attack on formal logic the 'law of identity' is singled out as an example of vacuous thought.

> It is asserted that the maxim of identity, though it cannot be proved, regulates the procedure of every consciousness, and that experience shows it to be accepted as soon as its terms are apprehended. To this alleged experience of the logic books may be opposed the universal experience that no mind thinks or forms conceptions or speaks, in accordance with this law, and that no existence of any kind whatever conforms to it. Utterances after the fashion of this pretended law (A Planet is a planet; Magnetism is magnetism; Mind is mind) are, as they deserve to be, reputed silly. That is certainly matter of general experience. The logic which seriously propounds such laws and the scholastic world in which alone they are valid have long been discredited with practical common sense as well as with the philosophy of reason.[13]

Again, in his *Science of Logic* Hegel argues that logical tautologies do not have a truth value, that in themselves they are nonsensical. The experience of hearing a tautological proposition is not one of obvious truth, but of obvious vacuity. In a passage which anticipates recent appeals to linguistic usage Hegel considers the bizarre role of tautologies in argument:

> When the question 'What is a plant?' is met by the answer 'A plant is a plant', the truth of this proposition is straightway admitted by the entire company upon which it is tested; and it will be said with equal unanimity that this answer says nothing. If one opens his mouth and promises to tell what

God is, namely, that God is - God, expectation is cheated, for it anticipated a different determination; and if this proposition is absolute truth, such absolute verbiage is held in exceedingly small esteem; nothing will be considered more boring and tedious than a conversation which still chews the same cud, or such speeches which are yet supposed to be truth.

If we consider more closely this tedious effect of such truths, we find that the beginning, 'A plant is - ', sets out to say something, to produce a further determination. But only a repetition is made, and the opposite has happened - nothing has been produced. Such idle talk is therefore self-contradictory.[14]

Identity has been held to serve as a foundational concept in the analysis of language, but, as Hegel argues, to begin merely with the assertion of identity is to say nothing and to assert anything determinate is to portray a grasp of identity and difference. Hegel makes a similar point concerning the so-called 'Law of Contradiction', which he describes as the 'negative form' of the Law of Identity, and concludes that both laws are 'not merely analytic, but synthetic'.[15]

The point Hegel is making can be clarified if we recognize that Hegel's logic embraces both the symbol and the object. As such, a table is not self-identical with itself but with the value bestowed upon it by a purposive human being. Both words and commodities take their meaning from social intercourse and cannot be apprehended abstractly. A logical contradiction, such as 'I am sad and I am not sad' or 'It is a plant and it is not a plant', appears as such only if we deliberately abstract their manifold richness in favour of the dull interpretation of the logician; that far from being the expressions of fundamental laws of reason, tautology and contradiction, formally conceived, are simply the frozen thought determinations of an excessive concern with meaning invariance.

Hegel is fully aware that both scientific and ordinary discourse constantly violates those laws of logic which philosophers have regarded as the essence of rationality. But does it follow that if two contradictory statements are expressed either one must be false or rational discourse must cease? Feyerabend offers an intriguing example relative to this point:

Watch a train leave the station through a window of your own compartment in an adjacent train. The train comes to a stop. You now see it (1) moving back into the station and (2) not changing place relative to the rim of your compartment window. The phenomenologically correct description of the process is that the train changes place and does not change place. There is an experience that is correctly described only by saying that **the same thing moves and does not move at the same time and in the same**

respect. The rule that a contradiction while fertile must still be removed would in this case advise us to give an incorrect description of an experience. There are of course ways of avoiding the problem. One can eliminate the contradiction-causing concepts and use others. But then we cease to have the experience that led to our problem for this experience depends precisely on the interplay of concepts and percepts. So, there is no way out: remove the contradiction and with it the experience of which it provides a phenomenologically adequate description or retain the contradiction and find better ways of dealing with contradictions than are provided by the formal logic of today.[16]

For Hegel, formal logic is 'abstract', 'lifeless', 'barren', and even 'boring'. He offers, by way of contrast, a logic manifesting a richness of content which surpasses anything that had previously been considered within the province of logic. Naturally aware that his reader, schooled in the formal tradition, will have difficulty, Hegel offers a justification of his approach.

The idea of life is concerned with a subject matter so concrete, and, if you will, so real that with it we may seem to have over-stepped the domain of logic as it is commonly conceived.[17]

It is not only the domain of logic that Hegel oversteps. His manipulation of teleological concepts and traditional distinctions pushes them to the point where they become virtually unrecognizable. In order to simplify matters we can, without any significant loss of meaning, substitute some of the key terms in Hegel's analysis of teleology. We can replace the term 'end' with 'skilled worker', since the latter represents a living end. Further simplification can be achieved if we replace 'syllogism' with 'purposive action', since Hegel's syllogisms represent a unity of thought and action in a reciprocal relationship between humans and nature and human social interaction. An Hegelian syllogism has three terms: a middle term (means, instrument, or slave) which mediates two extremes; an end (skilled worker or master); and an object (the raw material from which desires are satisfied). These relationships are far from static and at any given moment all three may interchange, with ends becoming means and the object becoming the end. We should also remember that, for Hegel, philosophy reflects on a dynamically changing social life and that his concept of teleology will itself reflect on the dramatic changes taking place in his world. Hegel is the philosopher of the Industrial Revolution. Foremost in his mind is the transition from an agrarian society to an industrial one. This, in turn, necessitates a different philosophical outlook. Hegel's philosophy contemplates a world no longer cut off from human agency, but a world that humans conquer as knowledge develops.

Consider how he speaks of the violence of the relationship between human beings and the world.

> This means is an object.... It is powerless against the end as it is against some other immediate object.[18]

In other words, the tool, or plough, is an object employed by the skilled worker against other objects which are powerless against it. Whilst objects may resist the power of a skilled worker, they are powerless against other objects which are employed by human intelligence. Hegel has an image of a violent interaction between humans and the world, whereby the former capture part of the mechanical world in order to use it against itself.

> Thus as against the end the object has the character of importance and subservience; the end is its subjectivity or soul which has its external side in the object.[19]

On the other hand the means has definite power over the external object. For it is the means which transforms the object in accord with the end desired by the skilled worker - the farmer's satisfaction is mediated by the plough. But the means, or instrument, has an immediate relationship to both extremes; to the farmer and to the land, the end and the external object. Against the farmer the plough is powerless, against the land it is powerful and violent.[20] This is not merely because it obeys causal laws but because it is operated by a human purpose. Says Hegel:

> In this relation its process is no other than the mechanical or chemical process ... but ... these processes pass back, through themselves, into the end.[21]

The image of violence suggests that this means-end relationship can be applied to human intercourse. For example:

> The way in which the end (the master) makes an object into the means (slave) may be considered violent.[22]

Here we find the logical structure of the master-servant dialectic outlined in the *Phenomenology of Spirit*. After a struggle which stops short of death the master uses the slave as a means for his own ends. Just as the plough mediates between the farmer and the harvest, so the master slides the slave between himself and the things he desires. He desires food without having to work for it. So he desires slavery and the means becomes an object of desire. The cotton plantation owners go to war for the defence of slavery. But the master becomes degraded and trapped in enjoyment, whilst the slave learns how to dominate the world and, in turn, how to dominate the master through the weakness of his desires. Thus it is ultimately through his attachment to things that the master loses his freedom.

At this point Hegel manifests greater foresight than Marx, for the Marxist desire for the universality of things need not lead to freedom, but to even greater enslavement. Slavery to the means of production may exist in the midst of undreamed of riches.

Now Kant objected to treating people as means, arguing that humans exist as ends in themselves. This is not entirely wrong but, as Hegel observed, in the real world such clear-cut distinctions are impossible to draw. Hegel could have been thinking of the French Revolution. The third estate, or middle term, was only a means for the *ancien régime* and, like the slave, sought to become everything. But events were to change and the means became the end and other groups were to emerge and saw it as a further means, and again ends became means and means became ends, until it became impossible to disentangle the multiple relationships and alliances in terms of the abstract dichotomies of Kantian philosophy. In human relationships the question 'Who is using whom?' is often too difficult to determine. Does the teacher use the student or the student use the teacher? Does the publisher use the author or the latter use the publisher? Or does the bookseller use them both? Is this immoral? Clearly not. In the real world it is impossible to draw a rigid distinction between instrument and end.

The question 'Who is using whom?' is raised by Hegel in the initial stages of the master-servant dialectic. He depicts two self-consciousnesses seeing each other as objects but refusing to grant mutual recognition as free autonomous persons. This theme has been developed by Sartre in *Being and Nothingness,* where he considers the experience of being an object for the other's 'look', and by R.D. Laing and the existential psychiatrists. In the writings of the latter, slave rebellion is a rejection of 'thinghood', a demand for recognition as free autonomous agents. But this is only part of what Hegel has to say and should not be seen as his explanation of how the slave overturns the power relationship. For whilst it may be essentially human to rebel against thinghood it is equally human to treat others as things and on certain occasions to expect to be treated as things. One cannot simply distinguish between a human being and a technical object and leave it at that. On numerous occasions it is of fundamental importance to exist as a thing. Human interaction in a gynaecological examination, for example, is primarily objective and technical in order to preserve the personal feelings and self-respect of the patient. 'As for exposure and manipulation of the patient's body', says Joan P. Emerson in an account of gynaecological examination, 'it would be a shocking and degrading invasion of privacy were the patient not defined as a technical object'.[23] Earlier in the same article she says: 'The staff want it understood their gazes take in only medically pertinent facts, so they are not concerned with an aesthetic inspection of a patient's body'.[24] Under the appropriate conditions, thinghood is essential to the maintenance of personality. But whilst it may be essential for medical activities to proceed it still constitutes an indignity at another level of reality. 'This', says Emerson, 'can be cancelled ... by simultaneously acknowledging the patient as a person'.[25] Thus a finely balanced alternation between seeing the patient as a person and as a thing expresses a multiple definition of reality which is only self-contradictory if one remains anchored to a logical gulf between things and personalities.

In the same way, Hegel recognizes that in human relationships the means-ends distinction can never be arrested; that human understanding often requires an alternation between being a means for others and an end for oneself. In fact, the fluidity of teleological concepts, like the reality they reflect, can be seen in a wide range of human relationships. But Hegel focuses his attention upon relationships arising out of the work process. So, returning to Hegel's account of the relationship between humans and nature, we find that the farmer desirous of the harvest also desires a ploughed field. From this rather obvious point Hegel constructs his account of the unity between finality and causality, contrasting his own position with Kant, for whom all 'production of material things takes place according to merely mechanical laws'. This, says Hegel, does not reflect the reality of human labour, where desires and nature's causality mutually affect each other. Furthermore, this interpenetration illustrates the progress of history through the various modes of production. Knowledge, political consciousness, and the scope for freedom are internally linked to the development of the productive forces, which are in turn reciprocally linked to human needs. Hegel's teleology is therefore progressive. One may begin with immediate ends, but these generate a new realm of ends and means, leading in turn to a broader and deeper understanding of nature: not simply a monotonous repetition of infinite progress but a 'constant self-reproduction of human society at a higher level'.[26] Rigid polarities between ends and means therefore collapse into a dialectical totality, and Hegel's teleology thus manifests a break with older teleologies and several contemporary strands of Marxism where ends are given undue significance and means sacrificed for either divine purpose or statist objectives.

III The Cunning of Man

Hegel often characterizes purposiveness in terms of cunning. In work the machine actualizes desire and the skilled worker employs his cunning when he allows nature to work itself out for him. He 'exposes it [the tool] as an object, allows it to exhaust itself, and surrendering it to attrition shields himself behind it from mechanical force'.[27] But if the machine takes on the role of a mechanical slave, what does the skilled worker do? He takes a rest. Occasionally he looks at his watch. Like the plough it too operates according to natural laws which do not cease to function when he is unconcerned with them. Sometimes Hegel has the skilled worker sitting in his house, having employed his knowledge of gravity to secure the roof, and his knowledge of fire to keep out the cold weather.[28] In *The Philosophy of History* Hegel extends this line of thought to draw an analogy between the natural and the social world.

> The building of a house is, in the first instance, a subjective aim and design. On the other hand we have, as means, the several substances required for the work - iron, wood, stones. The elements are made use of in working up this material: fire to melt the iron, wind to blow the fire, water to set wheels in motion, in order to cut the wood, etc. The result is, that the wind, which has helped to build the house, is shut out by the house; so also are the violence of rains and floods, and the destructive powers of fire, so far as the house is made fire-proof. The stones and beams obey the law of gravity - press downward - and so high walls are carried up. Thus the elements are made use of in accordance with their nature, and yet to co-operate for a product, by which their operation is limited. Thus the passions of men are gratified; they develop themselves and their aims in accordance with their natural tendencies, and build up the edifice of human society; thus fortifying a position for right and order **against themselves.**[29]

Nature's mechanism is utilized for human finality. The wind wears itself out in strengthening our defences against it. On its own, nature has no goals, but human beings, not God, put them there. As Marx says in a paraphrase of Hegel: 'An instrument of labour is a thing, or a complex of things, which the labourer interposes between himself and the subject of his labour'.[30] There can be little doubt that Hegel must have thought of the following verses from Sophocles's *Antigone* (lines 340-370) when formulating his account of the 'cunning' of man:

> Wonders are many on earth, and the greatest of these
> Is man, who rides the ocean and takes his way
> Through the deeps, through wind-swept valleys of perilous seas
>   That surge and sway.
>
> He is master of ageless Earth, to his own will bending
> The immortal master of gods by the sweat of his brow,
> As year succeeds to year, with toil unending
>   Of mule and plough.
>
> He is the lord of all things living; birds of the air,
> Beasts of the field, all creatures of sea and land
> He taketh cunning to capture and ensnare
>   With sleight of hand;

13

The use of language, the wind-swift motion of his brain
He learnt; found out the laws of living together
In cities, building him shelter against the rain
    And Wintry weather.

There is nothing beyond his power. His subtlety
Meeteth all chance, all danger conquereth.
For every ill he hath found its remedy,
    Save only death.

The power of humans, reflected in their employment of language, their cunning, reflected in the employment of natural forces to shield themselves from nature's violence, are all developed in Hegel's dialectic. And Hegel, like Sophocles and Marx, was unsatisfied with a static picture of the relationship between humans and nature, so he therefore characterizes a dramatic reversal. Although finality is essentially human, mechanism can nevertheless frustrate or, at least, divert human desire. The machine, too, has ends. Diamonds might be used to cut diamonds, robots might be used to make, mend, or control, robots, according to human desires, but this can be reversed. Just as the slave can become master, so the machine comes to impose its ends on the skilled worker. Says Hegel:

> In so far as the means is higher than the finite ends of external usefulness: the plough is more honourable than are immediately those enjoyments which are procured by it, and are ends. The instrument is preserved whilst the immediate enjoyments pass away and are forgotten. In his tools man possesses power over external nature, even though, according to his ends, he frequently is subjected to it.[31]

Just as the slave achieves universality at the master's expense, so the plough becomes more important than the harvest - the instrument becomes the end. To make ploughs one needs factories and industry. In making even better tools the process of industrialization is generated. This process is the outcome of human desires working in accord with nature's mechanism, but it develops according to its own logic. The controller becomes controlled by his own desires. The machine imposes its pattern and demands upon social life. Society is organized according to the needs of factory production. The skilled worker becomes a prisoner of the causal processes of production. It is easy to see how close all of this is to the *Economic and Philosophical Manuscripts* of the young Marx in 1844. Such dramatic reversals reflect on those curious ironies of history which Hegel describes as the 'cunning of reason', which refers to the process by which the intentional actions of human beings reveal a purpose other than that which was consciously intended. This doctrine has been severely criticized by Hegel's friends and foes alike. According to Lukács, it weakens Hegel's account of freedom, and contributes to his 'mystification of the historical process, his hypostatization of a "spirit" which acts as a conscious principle in which it is grounded'.[32] On these terms Hegel is saying that we are free only in so far as we act in accord with this cosmic spirit. But as Parkinson points out, Lukács is using the wrong model. The world spirit is not external to the actions of human beings.[33] We are not subjected to its powers as a falling stone is subject to the laws of gravity, or a stick caught up in a river. We might say that the current and the stick are externally related. But the world spirit is not distinct from the actions of individuals. On the contrary, Hegel's commitment to an internal teleology suggests that in so far as an individual acts he or she is part of the world spirit, and that the latter cannot be said to push individuals about.

Marx is often credited with debunking the Hegelian concept of a world spirit by showing that the powers attributed to God are really reified human powers. Without going too deeply into Hegel's theology, it is worth drawing attention to the fact that his reference to the absolute spirit (*der absolute Geist*) 'does not carry any existential implication; the definite article is attached to any abstract noun'.[34] To see Hegel's cunning of reason as an internal teleology is to call into question the view that history is stage-managed by some cosmic force. In an important respect Hegel's world spirit is the sum-total of unintended consequences and purposive action as seen through the eyes of the historian. To put it another way: we might say that the history of any civilization has a meaning which differs from the individual intentions of its constituent members. No matter how many consequences of an act may be foreseeable, any action or institution will have an indefinite number of side-effects. And even if **every** consequence were predictable, all would not be.

We can draw an analogy here with numbers: whilst we can count every whole number we cannot count all whole numbers. J.O. Wisdom has drawn attention to this point in another context, adding that 'unintended consequences may be **distributively** predictable but are not **collectively** predictable. All of which is just a logical way of bringing out the point that whatever effort we make to foresee unintended consequences and however successful we are, there must logically always be some we shall have failed to foresee'.[35] Unintended consequences that are not foreseen are logically similar to those which are foreseen, and do not have to stem from mysterious origins; they have the same origins as foreseen consequences, and may produce an overall state of affairs which no one in particular has intended. It is simply the result of the collections of individuals and institutions in history upon which historians impose intelligibility. As Hegel says in *Reason in History* :

> The realm of spirit consists in what is produced by man. One may have all sorts of ideas about the kingdom of God; but it is always a realm of spirit to be realized and brought about in man.[36]

And just as the internal relation between means and ends, between spirit and human agents, between the absolute and method, eschews an external agency, so the standard of rationality is internal to the various stages of historical development. In this sense, Hegel's slogan 'What is rational is actual and what is actual is rational' is not a plea for intellectual subservience to God or the temporal authorities, but a reference to the fact that the rationality of history is internally related to observations of the processes at work in history. Hegel's insistence that human beings obtain their notions of reason from their observations of the actual world is a rejection of both classical idealism and materialism.

Lukács is, of course, aware of Hegel's references to the 'cunning of man' and he draws attention to Hegel's remarks on government in this context.

> The cunning of government is to allow free reign to the self-interest of others - the right, the understanding of the merchant tells him what counts in the world: utility - the government must turn its **utility** to account and ensure that it returns back into the world. [37]

All of this suggests that the master-servant dialectic need not be tied exclusively to the triumph of the underdog. A government can retain its power by giving free reign to those subordinate to it. But in another sense the cunning is not merely the government's cunning, just as it is not merely the slave's or the cunning of some cosmic spirit: it is the rationality immanent in the conscious activity of the particular actions of the various social groups. Despite the obscureness of many of his arguments Hegel is as down-to-earth as Wittgenstein. The point of stressing the internality between the world spirit and the facts of history is to avoid the abstract distinction between the world as it is and the world as we know it. Distinctions between what we know and what we do not know fall within the world we can know - not in any transcendental sphere. There is no need to postulate another world independent of us, and there is no external absolute in the sense of an ultimate goal or cosmic purpose.

IV What Does Hegel Accomplish With His Concept of Teleology?

In the first place, it provides an understanding of objective reality which calls into question all external divisions between subject and object drawn by classical idealists and empiricists alike. For Hegel's account of reality is that of process and change which we come to understand as desire satisfying agents of change. He expresses this in logical terms, of syllogisms and of contradictions, but his approach must not be confused with formal logic or its alleged opposite, irrational emotionalism. It is a logic which expresses its content, and its content is to be found in the dialectic of labour, of purposive production. As Lukács says: 'Hegel's concrete analysis of the human labour process shows that the antinomy of causality and teleology is in reality a dialectical contradiction in which the laws governing a complex pattern of objective reality become manifest in motion, in the process of its own constant reproduction'.[38] To this end Hegel questions abstract distinctions between human beings and nature and is able to give an account of their relationship in progressive terms without lapsing into a romantic version of the lost harmony between human beings and nature and a consequential rejection of industrialism.

The fusion of causality and purpose is essential to Hegel's *Philosophy of Right,* where the abstract distinction between intention and act is called into question. The former, he argues, is not a mysterious subjective process which precedes operation of causal mechanisms. On the contrary, act and intention are fused, and moral evaluation cannot be applied exclusively to either the will or the performance: 'what the subject is, is the series of his actions. If these are a series of worthless productions, then the subjectivity of his willing is just as worthless. But if the series of his deeds is of a substantive nature, then the same is true also of the individual's inner will'.[39] The same point is made by Wittgenstein when he attributes moral guilt to the whole incident rather than to any subjective intention:

> 'I am not ashamed of what I did then, but of the intention which I had'. - And didn't the intention lie **also** in what I did? What justifies the shame? The whole history of the incident.[40]

Neither the physical act nor the intention alone can provide the moral content of an act. A murder is not merely a unit of action like the infliction of damage to flesh.[41] It includes a foreknowledge of the consequences and malicious intention. Having an intention is not merely having a subjective end in mind, it is explicable only in the context of the act and its institutional bearings.

In Hegel's concept of teleology one finds an abolition of the distinction between mechanist and purposive models of social explanation which has bewitched the social sciences for over a century. But of equal importance is his abolition of external distinctions between theory and practice, which he contrasts with a conception of reality that is internally linked to human labour. Finally, we have his novel reformulation of the relationship between freedom and necessity, where freedom is not abstract freedom from nature's causality but is determined by the ability to penetrate and exploit nature for a definite human purpose.

There is a natural progression from Hegel's teleology, with its emphasis upon productivity, to the materialist dialectics of Marx and Engels. The latter drew from Hegel's insights into the dialectic of labour when he spoke of the revenge of nature:

> If man, by dint of his knowledge and inventive genius, has subdued the forces of nature, the latter avenge themselves upon him by subjecting him, in so far as he employs them, to a veritable despotism independent of all social organization.[42]

Following Engels, both Lenin and Lukács have emphasized this development. Nevertheless, traces of mechanistic thought have survived and have been incorporated into Marxism. Whilst Marx emphasized the importance of class conflict for the transformation of social life, his classes were portrayed in mechanistic terms. The proletariat was presented as an exploited producing class which would, according to the logic of the productive forces, overturn the existing power structure. But Marx never saw the class struggle **within** the sphere of production. Seeing the worker as a passive object exploited for his labour power, Marx never considered the importance of the worker's resistance to production. The worker, in production, was seen as a passive means whose output and surplus-value could be objectively determined. As such the class struggle was depicted in terms of a struggle to reduce profits and increase wages. But as Hegel would have noticed, the history of industrial conflict is more than wage or profits disputes: it is also the history of resistance to production within the workplace. The industrialist does not buy an hour of passive labour as the Marxist model suggests; he buys an hour's output, which will vary according to the worker's resistance. In this sense, the worker is not a passive automaton, awaiting the birth of a new and freer society, but a person with a definite say in the determination of the exchange-value of labour power. In short: Marx's theory of pauperism was mechanistic in so far as it failed to consider the dialectical unity which Hegel had observed between nature's necessity and purposive freedom. To be sure, Marx's theory of pauperism is concerned with relative, not absolute pauperism, but even so, the **action** of social classes is neglected. Whilst factory production seeks to reduce the worker to a thing, it can never fully succeed without becoming dysfunctional. This, of course, is the lesson of Hegel's master-servant dialectic. Purposive behaviour and human freedom cannot be completely eradicated from the production process. Total mechanism, as Hegel argues, can never succeed until the death of the system in question.

Marx did, however, recognize that under certain conditions factory production generated contradictions. The more man creates machines, said Marx in his *Economic and Philosophical Manuscripts,* the more he is dominated and dehumanized by them. Such was the alienation which had its genesis in the division of labour in nineteenth-century factory production. But Marx saw this as a philosophical problem about which little could be done. If production were to continue in a communist society, a degree of alienation would remain. The realm of freedom, as Marx says in *Capital,* would be established outside of production. But what Marx sees as a philosophical contradiction is a literal one in a most profound sense. In the interests of greater productivity, under both capitalist and socialist systems, there is a **tendency** to reduce the labourer to the status of an artefact. But at the very same time, he is required to participate as a free and conscious human being, learning how to overcome the obstacles thrown up by the natural world, learning how to meet the resistance of the machine. Thus the logic of production generates an inescapable contradiction whereby the labourer is both excluded and included in the productive process. In simple terms, it is a contradiction between doing what one is told and doing one's job. If workers respond as automata - which they should do, according to the logic of production - the whole system will grind to a halt, which is exactly what happens in 'works to rule'. If people become passive objects they cannot produce. Yet if workers seek to control their own movements, initiate their own decisions, they pose a threat to the distribution of power within the institution. Every hour of every day, in factory or in office, hospital or school, employees live with this contradiction. It is a source of conflict within every factory, mine, office or hospital. In both socialist and capitalist societies, the worker is required to be both superman and automaton. It is to this much deeper realm of conflict in large-scale productive systems that Hegel's analysis of teleology is relevant. His questioning of the antithesis between mechanism and teleology calls for a re-examination of notions about human relations and natural laws which are embedded much deeper in the institutions of the industrial world than Marx or many of the historical materialists have envisaged.

Notes

1. Marx, K., *Capital,* vol. I, Progress, Moscow, 1961, p. 178.

2. Hobbes, T., *De Corpore,* English Works, vol. I, ed. W. Molesworth, London, 1839, p. 132.

3. *HSL,* vol. II, p. 375.

4. *HSL,* vol. II, pp. 440-1.

5. Hegel's *Jena Lectures,* cited by Georg Lukács, *The Young Hegel,* trans. R. Livingstone, Merlin Press, London, 1975, pp. 344-5.

6. Marx, *Capital,* vol. I, p. 177.

7. Engels, *Anti-Dühring,* Progress, Moscow, 1962, p. 157.

8. On the significance of Hegel's clues - the watch, the house, and the plough - I am deeply indebted to Jacques D'Hondt's 'Teleology and Praxis in Hegel's Logic', in *Hegel et la pensée moderne*, Paris, 1970, pp. 1-26. References to this work are from an unpublished translation by A.R. Manser.

9. Wittgenstein, L., *Tractatus Logico-Philosophicus*, Routledge & Kegan Paul, London, 1961, §3.334.

10. *HL*, §183.

11. Wittgenstein, *Philosophical Investigations*, Blackwell, Oxford, 1968, §486.

12. Wittgenstein, *On Certainty*, Blackwell, Oxford, 1969, §319.

13. *HL*, §115.

14. *HSL*, vol. II, p. 41.

15. *HSL*, vol. II, p. 42.

16. Feyerabend, P.K., 'In Defence of Aristotle', in *Progress and Rationality in Science*, edited by G. Radnitzky and G. Andersson, D. Reidel, Dordrecht, 1978, p. 157.

17. *HSL*, vol. II, p. 401.

18. *HSL*, vol. II, p. 385.

19. *HSL*, vol. II, pp. 385-6.

20. *HSL*, vol. II, pp. 386-7.

21. *HSL*, vol. II, p. 387.

22. *HSL*, vol. II, p. 387.

23. Emerson, Joan P., 'Behavior in Private Places: Sustained Definition of Reality in Gynecological Examinations', in *Recent Sociology*, no. 2, edited by Hans Peter Dreitzel, Macmillan, New York, 1970, p. 79.

24. Ibid., p. 78.

25. Ibid., p. 80.

26. Lukács, op. cit., p. 348.

27. *HSL*, vol. II, p. 387.

28. D'Hondt, op. cit., pp. 7–8.

29. *PH*, p. 27.

30. Marx, *Capital*, vol. I, p. 197.

31. *HSL*, vol. II, p. 388.

32. Lukács, op. cit., p. 357.

33. Parkinson, G.H.R., 'Hegel's Concept of Freedom', Royal Institute of Philosophy Lectures, vol. 5, *Reason and Reality*, Macmillan, London, 1972, p. 189.

34. Manser, A.R., 'Critical Notice', *Mind*, vol. 87, no. 345 (1978), p. 122.

35. Wisdom, J.O., 'Situational Individualism and the Emergence of Group Properties', in *Explanation in the Behavioural Sciences*, edited by R. Borger and F. Cioffi, Cambridge University Press, 1970, pp. 275–6.

36. *RH*, p. 20.

37. Hegel's *Jenenser Realphilosophie*, vol. II, p. 262, cited by Lukács, op. cit., p. 355.

38. Lukács, op. cit., p. 346.

39. *HPR*, §124.

40. *Philosophical Investigations*, Blackwell, Oxford, 1968, §644.

41. Ibid., §119.

42. Engels, F., 'On Authority', in *The Marx-Engels Reader*, second edition, edited by Robert Tucker, W.W. Norton, New York, 1978, pp. 731–2.

2 The Mediating Role of Estates and Corporations in Hegel's Theory of Political Representation

BERNARD CULLEN

For Allen Wood

I Introduction

It is well known that Hegel's mature theory of ethical life or practical social ethics (*die Sittlichkeit*) is divided into three aspects or levels: (i) the family (*die Familie*); (ii) civil society (*die bürgerliche Gesellschaft*); and (iii) the state (*der Staat*). Hegel charts a dialectical development within ethical life, from the natural and relatively unreflective universality of the family into the subjective particularity of civil society, a development which culminates in the fully actualized unity of universality and particularity in the state.

Civil society is the sphere of particularity (*Besonderheit*), the realm of 'the concrete person, who is himself the object of his particular aims' (§182); 'its specific end is ... the security and protection of property and personal freedom' (§258R).[1] Civil society is the socio-economic expression of 'the self-subsistent inherently infinite personality of the individual, the principle of subjective freedom' (§185R). It is the economic *bellum omnium contra omnes,* 'the battlefield where everyone's individual private interest meets everyone else's' (§289R), where each self-seeking individual is primarily absorbed in satisfying his or her own selfish ends, without respect for the common good.

But civil society also manifests an element of universality, since 'the particular person is essentially so related to other particular persons that each establishes himself and finds satisfaction by means of the others' (§182). Particularity is gradually mediated, as it becomes clear that the pursuit of private selfish ends is governed by the general laws of political economy. Individuals come to see how 'the livelihood, happiness, and legal status of each [*die Subsistenz und das Wohl des Einzelnen und sein rechtliches Dasein*] is interwoven with the livelihood, happiness and rights of all' (§183). In this sense, civil society is a 'system of complete interdependence [*System allseitiger Abhängigkeit*]' (§183). This interdependence, however, is based on the purely selfish motive of need satisfaction:

in civil society each individual is his own end [*ist jeder sich Zweck*], everything else is nothing to him. But except in contact with others he cannot attain the whole compass of his ends, and these others and his relations with them are merely means to the end of the particular individual [*Mittel zum Zweck des Besondern*].[2]

Civil society is merely 'the external state, the state based on need, the state as the understanding envisages it [*als den äußeren Staat - Not- und Verstandesstaat*]' (§183). The 'particular' individual regards 'the universal' (that is, true community of purpose) as something distinct or alien. A synthesis of particularity and universality - the culmination of Hegel's dialectical description of social reality - is achieved only when the latter is internalized in the consciousness of free individuals, within the reasonable modern state.[3]

Civil society is the realm of subjective particularity: 'In civil society, the Idea [*die Idee*] is lost in particularity and has fallen asunder with the separation of inner and outer' (§229). 'The Idea' is the subject-matter of Hegel's whole philosophical system - the totality of human experience - a segment of which he is describing in his *Rechtsphilosophie*. Generally speaking, 'the Idea' is the all-encompassing synthesis of subject (the inner) and object (the outer), of particularity and universality; in the context of ethical life, 'the Idea' is the synthesis of the freedom of the private individual and the public demands of the community, a synthesis to be found only in the state that conforms to the principles of reason.

Within civil society, on the other hand, in which the forces of unfettered individualism and economic competition are unleashed, a gap appears between the two components of this synthesis. The members of civil society see the state as an alien power intent on restricting their individual freedom; they carry on their self-seeking activities in the economic field. Although the institutionalization of the division of labour fosters a general awareness of the mutual interdependence of the free individuals in civil society, this lowest level of social integration is still quite inadequate. The process of integration is advanced through the administration of justice and through the agency of 'the public authority [*die Polizei*]'. The actions of the public authority satisfy the demand that 'the undisturbed safety of the person and property be attained; and that the securing of every individual's livelihood and well-being be treated and actualized as a right' (§230). Complete unity of universality and particularity is, however, only possible in the state as Hegel conceives it. And a truly reasonable state must have institutions that bring these elements together in a dialectical unity that retains the full force of the two poles: individual freedom preserved within a political community. Hegel proceeds to describe the social institutions that facilitate the necessary process of integration or mediation. The most important of these institutions - because they straddle the division between private economic activity and public political activity - are the estates and the corporations. The isolated, free individual can be integrated into the harmonious social totality only by identifying with a specific estate, and by becoming a member of a corporation.

The major challenge of Hegel's philosophical politics, then, is to integrate the self-subsistent free individuals of civil society into the political institutions of the state:

> particularity by itself is measureless and excessive [das Maaßlose, das Ausschweißende].... The whole order [die Ganzheit] must at the same time retain strength enough to put particularity in harmony with the unity of ethical life [mit der sittlichen Einheit].[4]

He does this by describing an organic political constitution in which the citizens of the state (that is to say, the individuals in civil society) can participate. In the remainder of this essay, I propose to analyse Hegel's strategies for integrating isolated individuals into the ethical community of the state, especially his understanding of the role of the estates and the corporations in the system of political representation.[5] Finally, I shall examine briefly some of the implications of Hegel's theory of representation for contemporary politics.

II The Estates

The very first stage of mediation (Vermittelung) between individuals as members of civil society and as citizens in the state is work, the means whereby individual needs are satisfied: 'the means [die Vermittelung] of preparing and acquiring the particularized means appropriate to our similarly particularized needs is work [die Arbeit]' (§196). The resulting subdivision of needs and means to their satisfaction prompts the refinement of skills through practical education, which in turn leads to the subdivision of production and the division of labour (die Teilung der Arbeiten) (§198).

Hegel is no egalitarian, and he insists on 'the natural inequality of people [die von der Natur ... gesetzte Ungleichheit der Menschen] (§200R), since civil society retains within itself 'the arbitrary particularity of nature [die natürliche als willkürliche Besonderheit]' (§200R). Reason, however, arranges the differences within 'this sphere of particularity', with its 'disparities of individual

24

resources [*Vermögens*] and skills [*Geschicklichkeiten*]' into 'an organic whole [*zu einem organischen Ganzen von Unterschieden gliedert*]' (§200R). Within the whole complex of civil society, with its infinitely diverse needs, means of satisfaction, and related types of work, individual members are constrained to fall into general vocational groups or estates (*zu einem Unterschiede der Stände*) (§201).

Hegel names these estates as follows:

(i)   the substantial (or agricultural) estate;
(ii) the formal (or business) estate; and
(iii) the universal estate (of civil servants) (§202).

The business estate (*der Stand des Gewerbs*) is further subdivided, according to the individual's occupational activities, into:

(a)   *der Handwerksstand* - the category devoted to craftsmanship;
(b)   *der Fabrikantenstand* - those involved in mass production in factories; and
(c)   *der Handelsstand* - those engaged in commerce (§204).

The distribution of individuals among estates and sub-estates is determined by one's occupation, which in turn is partly determined by the needs of the society, but also by the particular preferences and abilities of individuals:

> The question of the particular estate to which an individual is to belong is one on which natural capacity, birth and other circumstances have an influence, but the final and essential determining factors are subjective opinion and the individual's arbitrary will [*in der besondern Willkür*] (§206).

Belonging to an estate is an integral part of the process of 'mediating oneself with the universal, as well as gaining recognition both in one's own eyes and in the eyes of others [*in seiner Vorstellung und der Vorstellung Anderer anerkannt zu sein*]' (§207). The most important point, however, is that an individual can give up his or her isolation only by becoming a member of an estate:

> The individual actualizes himself [*gibt sich Wirklichkeit*] only by actually coming into being, thus becoming something specifically particularized; this means restricting oneself exclusively to one of the particular spheres of need (§207).

Becoming a member of a specific estate is part of becoming a fully human person.

III The Corporations

The other crucial mediating link between the egoism of civil society and personal identification with the common good in the state is the corporation. Hegel underlines its importance when he remarks that

> as the family was first, so the corporation is the second ethical root of the state, the one planted in civil society (§255).... The sanctity of marriage and the dignity of corporation membership [*die Ehre der Korporation*] are the two fixed points [*Momente*] round which the unorganized atoms [*die Desorganisation*] of civil society revolve (§255R).

If it were not for the family and the corporations (according to this metaphor), the individual members of civil society would fly off in all directions. Corporation membership is not considered necessary for everyone in civil society, all the same: the agricultural estate and the bureaucracy both have strong universal elements, each in its own way. However, 'the estate between them, the business estate [*der Stand des Gewerbes*], is essentially concentrated on the particular, and hence it is to it that corporations are specially appropriate' (§250). Because the business estate is essentially devoted to selfish economic pursuits, it stands in special need of moral socialization.

Again, corporation membership is primarily determined according to occupation: in a corporation, individuals who share some common economic or vocational bond (members of the various professions, entrepreneurs, tradesmen) come together to form an organization to represent their common interest. This is a crucial step in integrating the many competing economic interests of the individuals in civil society: 'the implicit likeness of such particulars to one another becomes really existent as what they share in common in an association [*als Gemeinsames in der Genossenschaft*]' (§251). It should be emphasized that Hegel is **not** referring here to the modern trade union, since trade unions are meant to represent the interests of employees in opposition to those of employers. It becomes clear that Hegel sees the corporation (as an economic association) as representing the interests of employers in a particular industry, or of self-employed members of a given industry or profession (such as the Federation of Engineering Employers, the British and American Medical Associations, or the Incorporated Law Society): associations such as these exercise effective control over their own industry or profession, through strict monitoring of entry and vigorous lobbying of government. The economic functions of Hegel's corporations are broadly those of the medieval guild, as he intimates when he laments 'the abolition of corporations in recent times'.[6] While recognizing that the old system of guilds degenerated and became ossified, he argues that a properly supervised system of corporations need not place crippling restrictions on freedom of business.[7] Under the heading of corporations, however, Hegel includes not just economic associations, but also other groups such as religious congregations (see §270R), communities of residents, municipalities, etc.

Although the members of corporations come together primarily to further their own individual interests (a quite legitimate motive within civil society),

> a selfish purpose, directed towards its particular self-interest, simultaneously apprehends and evinces itself as universal; all members of civil society are in virtue of their own particular skills members of a corporation, whose universal purpose is thus wholly concrete and no wider in scope than the purpose involved in business, its proper concerns and interests (§251).

Hegel's point here is that the purpose of a given corporation is universal to the extent that the benefits of membership accrue to **all** its members; and it is recognized that the individual member 'is actively interested in promoting the disinterested aim of that whole' (§253). Furthermore, individuals come to recognize that they 'belong to a whole that is itself a part of the general society' (§253). All the same, the element of universality is still far from adequate, since the benefits accrue only to the members of that particular corporation and not to society as a whole.

Membership of a corporation helps to give individuals a sense of their own identity: 'the member of a corporation needs no further external marks as evidence of his income and subsistence, i.e. that he is a somebody [*daß es etwas ist*]' (§253). Here Hegel provides an insight into the type of members of civil society he sees as candidates for corporation membership (even though he had said above that **all** members of civil society are members of a corporation). He now uses the term *Klasse,* which he reserves solely to denote sub-groups within the business estate, when he refers to 'the luxury of the business classes and their passion for extravagance [*Luxus und Verschwendungssucht der gewerbtreibenden Klassen*]' (§253R). It is not clear exactly whom these 'business classes' include; the adjective *gewerbtreibend* could refer to anyone in business, either industry or commerce, but the reference to their luxury and extravagance clearly suggests that they are relatively wealthy industrialists and businessmen. Hegel insists that 'this phenomenon has an ethical ground [*sittliche Grund*]' (§253R). Presumably this is because the pursuit of self-interest is quite legitimate within civil society, the sphere of particularity. But Hegel's argument becomes difficult to follow at this point.

> Unless he is a member of an authorized corporation [*einer berechtigten Korporation*], ... an individual is without professional rank [*ohne Standesehre*], and is reduced through his isolation to the merely selfish aspect of business [*auf die selbstsüchtige Seite des Gewerbs*] (§253R).[8]

Consequently (*'somit'*, says Hegel, but I am not overly impressed by the line of argument), he will try to gain recognition for himself as a person by acquiring the trappings of wealth. People involved in a business have the right to make money and acquire 'external proofs of their success in business [*die äußerlichen Darlegungen seines Erfolgs in seinem Gewerbe*], to which proofs no limits can be set' (§253R).

The corporations, however, also have a role to play in the moral development of their members. The pursuit of self-interest is mitigated within the corporation, and 'rectitude [*die Rechtschaffenheit*] obtains there its proper recognition and respect' (§253R). This is because the corporation member acquires duties towards his fellow members, such as the corporate provision of welfare; and thus 'wealth ceases to inspire either pride or envy, pride in its owners, envy in others' (§253R).[9]

IV The Assembly of Estates

In the third and final section of his account of *die Sittlichkeit* , Hegel analyses the state under three headings: (a) constitutional or domestic law (*das innere Staatsrecht*); (b) international law (*das äußere Staatsrecht*); and (c) world history (*die Weltgeschichte*). Within the element of the domestic law devoted to the domestic constitution (*innere Verfassung für sich*), he details its three components: (i) the monarchy (*die fürstliche Gewalt*); (ii) the executive (*die Regierungsgewalt*); and (iii) the legislature (*die gesetzgebende Gewalt*).

Corporations have a minor but important role to play in carrying out the decisions of the monarch and the executive and in maintaining the laws at a local level. This is because 'particular interests which are common to everyone fall within civil society and lie outside the absolutely universal interest of the state proper' (§288). Hegel here includes among corporations those of 'communities and other businesses and estates [*Korporationen der Gemeinden und sonstiger Gewerbe und Stände*]' (§288). These corporations (some of which correspond very roughly to our contemporary institutions of local government) can function authoritatively because of the confidence held in them by their peers and the general citizenry. But the interests of the corporations must ultimately be subordinated to the higher interests of the state, and to this end positions of responsibility in corporations will generally be filled by a mixture of public election by those who have an interest and appointment by higher authority (§288).[10] The corporations also serve to keep in check, from below, the power of ministers and their officials (§295), as well as helping to ensure that 'the middle estate of civil servants and members of government' does not 'acquire the isolated position of an aristocracy and use its education and skill as means to an arbitrary tyranny' (§297). In this respect, the corporations are the representatives (in modern parlance) of 'grass-roots opinion'.

The most crucial role of the estates and the corporations is the part they play in Hegel's system of political representation. Hegel's domestic constitution is made up of three elements: the monarchy, the executive, and the legislative authority, the Assembly of Estates (*das ständische Element*).[11] The Assembly of Estates has the function of bringing into the decision-making of the state 'the opinions and thoughts of the many [*der Vielen*]' (§301).

Through the medium of the estates, 'the subjective moment in universal freedom, the private judgement and the private will of the sphere called in this book civil society', is integrated into the fabric of the state (§301R).

> Regarded as a mediating organ [*als vermittelndes Organ betrachtet*], the Assembly of Estates stands between the government in general on the one hand and the people [*dem Volke*] broken up into particular spheres and individuals on the other (§302).

It must possess a feeling for administration and government; but also for the interests of particular groups and individuals. It is a mediating link (*eine Vermittelung*) between the power of the prince and the particular interests of societies, corporations and individuals. Most important of all, says Hegel (ever fearful of the destructive potential of the mob), the Assembly of Estates

> prevents individuals from having the appearance of a mass [*einer Menge*] or an aggregate [*eines Haufens*], and so from acquiring an organized opinion and volition and from crystallizing into a powerful bloc in opposition to the organized state (§302).

Among the estates of civil society, the universal estate (the estate of civil servants) is excluded from participation in the legislature, since it is essentially concerned with universal affairs. In the legislative Assembly of Estates (*in der ständischen Elemente der gesetzgebenden Gewalt*), 'the private estate [*der Privatstand*] acquires its political significance and efficacy' (§303).[12] The Assembly of Estates is divided into two chambers. One represents the agricultural estate, the estate 'more particularly fitted for political position and significance', which is 'summoned and entitled to its political vocation by birth without hazards of election' (§307).[13]

The other chamber is made up of the representatives of the business estate, 'the fluctuating element [*die bewegliche Seite*] of civil society' (§308), the estate based on 'particular needs and the work whereby these are met' (§303). This element can enter the political realm only through its deputies (*Abgeordnete*). This is partly because its members are so numerous; but more importantly because its activities are essentially individualistic. Thus, the representatives to the second chamber are chosen in accordance with 'the already constituted associations, communities, and corporations [*Genossenschaften, Gemeinden und Korporationen*], which in this way acquire a connection with politics' (§308). Hegel refines this point a couple of pages later, when he says that 'owing to the nature of civil society, the deputies [*die Abordnung*] come from its various corporations' (§311). The constituencies of the second chamber, therefore, are preeminently the corporations of civil society; and the deputies are to be drawn from their number. This is so that the deputies should be 'familiar with and themselves participate in its special needs, difficulties, and particular interests' (§311). On the basis of this, Hegel concludes that since 'the choice of deputies thereby complies with all points of view [*in civil society*], their election [*Wählen*] either is actually somewhat superfluous or is reduced to a trivial play of opinion and arbitrariness' (§311). Although he does not unambiguously declare that there should be **no** elections, Hegel makes it clear that he is not terribly keen on elections to the legislature.[14]

He makes it equally clear that not everyone is to be involved in this political process. He had earlier declared the function of the Assembly of Estates to be the integration into the state of the opinions and thoughts of the many (§301). He underlines the fact that he does mean 'the many' (*die Vielen* , οἱ πολλοί) and not **Alle.** If it is obvious that this 'all' does not include children or mere women (*Weiber*), he argues, then just as obviously 'the many' is the proper term. He ridicules the widespread notion that the deputies from the people (*aus dem Volk*), or even the people themselves, must know best what is in their own best interest. The fact is, he insists, that 'the people' - if by that term is meant a particular section of the members of a state - designates precisely that section which does **not** know what it wants:

> to know what one wants, and even more to know what the absolute will, reason, wants, is the fruit of profound knowledge [*Erkenntnis*] and insight [*Einsicht*] - precisely the qualities that 'the people' does not have (§301R).[15]

Indeed, much of this section consists of a tirade against the preposterous notion that 'the so-called people [*das sogenannte Volk*]' should have a direct political input:

> To hold that every single person should share in deliberating and deciding on general affairs of state on the grounds that all individuals are members of the state, and that its affairs are their affairs, and that it is right that what is done should be done with their knowledge and volition, is tantamount to a proposal to put the democratic element without any reasonable form [*ohne alle vernünftige Form*] into the

30

organization of the state, although it is only in virtue of the possession of such a reasonable form that the state is an organism at all (§308R).

The 'reasonable form' that is necessary for actual membership of the state (as opposed to 'being a member of the state' considered abstractly) is, as Hegel has already intimated, articulation into the estates and corporations:

> The concrete state is the whole, arranged into its particular groups [*Kreise*]; the member of a state is a member of such an estate [*Stand*], and it is only as characterized in this objective way that he can be considered when we are dealing with the state.... Hence the individual attains his actual and living determination [*Bestimmung*] only when he becomes a member of a corporation, a community, etc. (§308R).

Hegel also dismisses as absurd (*abgeschmackt*) the notion that everyone can understand what's going on in affairs of state. All the same, he says, 'public opinion [*öffentliche Meinung*]' is there for anyone who wants to sound off with their own 'subjective opinion' on such matters.

Hegel insists that the position of deputy requires several specific qualifications. The only way to ensure that deputies have the necessary qualifications and experience for successful public office is to restrict appointment to those in civil society who have demonstrated a proven sense of authority (*erprobten obrigkeitlichen Sinn*) in their business dealings (§310). For this a property qualification (*die Eigenschaft des Vermögens*) is a useful guide (§310R). Furthermore, it is important that each of the main branches of society should be represented in the second chamber by deputies who are thoroughly conversant with it and who themselves belong to it: 'e.g. deputies for trade, for manufacturing industry, etc. [*für den Handel, für die Fabriken usf.*]' (§311R).

According to Hegel, then, the second chamber of the legislature is to be composed of experienced and respected (and more or less wealthy) leading members of corporations, to represent the interests of the various sub-estates within the business estate of civil society. When he emphasizes that 'unless he is a member of an authorized corporation, ... an individual is without professional rank [*ohne Standesehre*], he is reduced through his isolation to the merely selfish aspect of business, and his livelihood and satisfaction become insecure' (§253R), his point is not simply an economic one, but primarily an ethical one. Remember that 'the sanctity of marriage and the dignity of corporation membership [*die Ehre der Korporation*] are the two fixed points round which the unorganized atoms [*die Desorganisation*] of civil society revolve' (§255R). Hegel insists that there must be an appropriate organization which the isolated individual member of civil society can join: 'In our modern states, the particular citizens [*die besondern Bürger*] have only a restricted share in the general business of the state, yet it is essential to present ethical individuals [*sittlichen Menschen*] with general activity, with the management of public interests [*eine allgemeine Tätigkeit, eine Besorgung des allgemeinen Interesses*], apart from their private business.... This work of a public character is found in a corporation'.[16] The corporation is the crucial middle term permitting the isolated self-seeking individual to initiate the process of integration into the community as a whole. Corporations mediate (on one level) between the isolated individuals and civil society at large, and then (as the corporations are represented in the Assembly of Estates) between the organized members of civil society and the state. But individuals who are not members of a corporation are alienated from participation in the universality of the state: 'it is in the corporation that activity for the community [*für ein Allgemeines*] becomes fully known [*ist eine Gewußte*]'.[17]

When we refer back to Hegel's earlier discussion of the corporations, however, we see just how restrictive he means corporation membership to be. He specifically stipulates that the businessman who is eligible for membership of a corporation 'is different from the day-labourer [*der Gewerbsmann ist verschieden vom Tagelöhner*], or from someone who is prepared to undertake casual employment on a single occasion. The former, who is, or will become, a master [*Meister*], is a member of the association not for casual gain on single occasions but for the whole range, the universality, of his particular livelihood' (§252R).[18] That is, the corporation member must have a skill and the reasonable expectation of a 'regular income and subsistence' (§253). The class of those who sell their labour for wages seems to be excluded from membership of a corporation. It is unthinkable that Hegel was including wage-labourers among the 'masters' or even potential 'masters'. In fact, he specifically draws attention to 'the dependence and need of the class tied to that kind of [*factory*] work [*die Abhängigkeit und Not der an diese Arbeit gebundenen Klasse*]' (§243).[19] Since wage-labourers are constantly at the mercy of the forces of the labour market and may be dismissed at any time (especially in Hegel's day, when contracts of manual work would have been unheard of), they could certainly not be said to enjoy 'a regular income and subsistence'. The logic of Hegel's analysis is inescapable: those who work for wages are deemed ineligible for corporation membership, and they are thereby excluded from political participation in the Assembly of Estates.

V Some Contemporary Implications

To the extent that the working class is not integrated into the social order of the state through membership of appropriate corporations, Hegel's project is a failure. Strictly in terms of his own detailed sociological descriptions of the conflicting forces within civil society

- conflicts which are not satisfactorily overcome (*aufgehoben*) in the *Philosophy of Right* - the state is not, as he claims, a unified and harmonious totality. His own description of the institutions of the reasonable modern state is not fully consistent in all its details; and some of his dialectical transitions stretch both logic and the imagination. But that is by no means the end of the story. In my account of Hegel's theory of estates and corporations, I have sought to extrapolate and elucidate the **philosophical** principles underpinning his system of social and political mediation, while at the same time drawing attention to the problems highlighted by Hegel's application of those principles to the socio-economic conditions of his own day. The problems of civil society are real and persistent; some of them are indeed glaring. But in my view they are essentially of a sociological or empirical rather than a philosophical order, and the underlying philosophical model of social life escapes relatively unscathed.

The central problem of Hegel's social and political philosophy is to harmonize the apparently conflicting interests of the individual and the community of which he or she is a member, and to delineate the social and political institutions which permit private individuals to be integrated into the social totality without sacrificing their privacy and freedom. This problem is perhaps the central political problem; it is certainly at least as pressing today as it was in Hegel's day. Riots, terrorism, very low turnouts at elections, all point to widespread disaffection with the political process throughout the developed world.

Hegel's solution - his philosophical theory of social and political mediations - is an application to social life of his logic, and this theory cannot be properly understood and appreciated if it is wrenched from the general framework of his logical categories. His declaration (in the Preface) that 'the whole, like the formation of the parts, rests on the logical spirit' (*HPR*, p. 2) must be taken to heart. His claim that 'the speculative way of knowing [*diese spekulative Erkenntnisweise*]' is distinctive is correct: this is indeed what is distinctive about the *Philosophy of Right*, which provides the social content for Hegel's otherwise empty logical categories. To accuse Hegel of distorting social realities in order to squeeze them into his logical categories is to miss the point here. Hegel insisted that he was merely **describing** the institutions of mediation present in the modern state. They may not be fully developed in any one state, but they are present all the same (in embryo, at least), more or less imperfectly. Hegel did not invent them.[20] To this extent, his work is indeed descriptive. But he also considered it to be an essential part of the mission of the conscientious philosopher to articulate the presence and function of these institutions, to draw attention to their crucial role in society, and to encourage their development. Hegel made it clear that a state which did not develop good political institutions was not as good a state (not as reasonable [*vernünftig*]) as one which did. In this sense, his work is unashamedly prescriptive. But I see no contradiction in this.

33

It is certainly not necessary to accept Hegel's metaphysics of the absolute in order to appreciate the enduring value of his political philosophy. What is required is to retain Hegel's basic philosophical principle of the dialectical mediation of the Many in the One, while not concerning oneself too much about the contingencies of early nineteenth-century social and political conditions and prejudices. For example, Hegel certainly recognized the problem of the undifferentiated masses (workers and the rabble of paupers). Profoundly affected by the actions of the mob in the wake of the French Revolution, he was ever fearful of the destructive potential of 'a powerful bloc [*bloß massenhaften Gewalt*] in opposition to the organic state' (§302). As we have seen above (p. 30), his invective against 'the so-called people' and their champions is particularly withering in the *Philosophy of Right*.[21]

By the time he came to lecture on the state again in 1823, however, he implied that some means would have to be found to organize 'the people' into an organ of the state: 'When the multitude enters the state as one of its organs, it achieves its interests by legal and orderly means. If these means are not available, the voice of the masses will always be for savagery [*wird das Aussprechen der Masse immer ein Wildes sein*]'.[22] He is even more forthright in his 1825 lectures. He points out that hitherto the main priority has been to organize assemblies and estates, from above.

> But the lower classes, the mass of the population [*das Untere, das Massenhafte des Ganzen*] are easily left more or less unorganized, and it is of the utmost importance that they be organized, because only so do they acquire strength, power [*Macht, Gewalt*]. Otherwise they are only a multitude, a heap of fragmented atoms [*ein Haufen, eine Menge von zersplitterten Atomen*], a heap with no power of reason [*keine vernünftige Gewalt*], a blind strength. Legitimate power [*berechtigte Gewalt*] will only be achieved when the particular spheres have been organized.[23]

Hegel himself could not suggest specific ways in which 'the lower classes' could be organized; he could not bring himself (for reasons, good or bad, outlined above) to include them among the corporations. In that sense, the problem defeated him. His own account of the workings of civil society and the various mechanisms of social integration is vitiated largely by the patronizing attitudes to simple working people that were an accidental rather than an essential feature of the times in which he lived. But the essential point - which retains its validity and force - is that the basic social entity is the totality, which he calls the organic state. In seeking to understand our social lives (and in seeking to make our social arrangements work better), we must begin with the whole, rather than with its constituent individuals. If we begin with the autonomous individuals (the dominant tradition in English-language political philosophy for 300 years), we shall never succeed in putting the pieces of the jigsaw together.

The political jurisdiction in which individuals live must be seen by them as a special kind of unity of which they are an integral part, to which they belong, to which they are ethically (*sittlich*) committed, and in which they participate politically. The relationship between the individual and the state (the state considered not just as the political superstructure but as the social totality) is not possible, according to Hegel, without intermediary institutions to which the individual gives allegiance. Different countries will have different types of institutions, in accordance with their particular traditions and conditions; and there will be different mediating institutions appropriate to different categories of citizen. Although Hegel calls these mediating institutions corporations, we need not follow him in this. But the principle of mediation, as bequeathed by Hegel, remains an indispensable tool of political philosophy.[24]

Notes

I am deeply indebted to Allen Wood, for introducing me many years ago to the *Philosophy of Right* and for guiding me through its riches with such clarity and insight. I am also grateful to those members of the Hegel Society of Great Britain (especially Zbigniew Pelczynski and Michael Petry) who offered helpful comments on an earlier version of this essay presented to the Society's Seventh Annual Conference in Oxford in September 1985; and to those who offered comments on the version presented at Boston College in September 1986. My interpretations remain, of course, my own responsibility.

1. Numbers in the text refer to numbered paragraphs in the published *Philosophy of Right* of 1820; numbers followed by R refer to 'remarks' subjoined to those paragraphs. While finding Knox's translation (*HPR*) generally invaluable, I often depart from it, preferring a more literal rendering of Hegel's text. I also include quotations from the transcripts by Heinrich Hotho (1822/23) and K.J. von Griesheim (1824/25) of Hegel's lecture courses on *Rechtsphilosophie*, published by Karl-Heinz Ilting as volumes 3 and 4 respectively of his edition of Hegel's *Vorlesungen über Rechtsphilosophie* [1818-1831], Frommann-Holzboog, Stuttgart-Bad Cannstatt, 1973-4. These transcripts were plundered by Hegel's disciple Eduard Gans to make up what he called the *Zusätze* to his 1833 and 1854 editions of the *Philosophie des Rechts*. These latter, translated by Knox as 'additions' to the main text, must be treated with circumspection, not because they are not 'authentic' Hegel texts (I believe, with Ilting, that the transcripts are almost verbatim accounts of Hegel's lectures, delivered, we are told by his

listeners, at dictation speed), but because the Gans version is a conflation of excerpts from two sets of lectures, and is often a loose paraphrase of them (an 'improved version') into the bargain! The Ilting edition is the only reliable one. I cite it henceforth as 'Ilting' followed by the volume number.

2. Ilting 3, p. 567; cf. *HPR,* addition to §182, p. 267.

3. 'This treatise', says Hegel of the *Philosophy of Right,* 'which contains the science of the state, is to be nothing other than the endeavour to apprehend and portray the state as something inherently reasonable [*als ein in sich Vernünftiges*]' (Preface, *HPR,* p. 11). It is a pity that Knox systematically translates *vernünftig* as 'rational', and that this habit has passed into the literature, especially since the substantive *die Vernunft* is always translated as 'reason'. The terms 'rational' and 'rationality' (and, as every university lecturer should well know, 'rationalization'), as generally used in this century, are redolent of the analytical and instrumental rationality of the Enlightenment that Hegel labels, with some disdain, 'the tabulating understanding [*der tabellarische Verstand*]'. See my discussion of the distinction in part II of 'Hegel's historical phenomenology and social analysis', in D. Lamb (ed.), *Hegel and Modern Philosophy,* Croom Helm, London and Sydney, and St. Martin's Press, New York, 1987, pp. 1-29; cf. Otto Pöggeler, 'Rationality, or art in the world of technology', in *Irish Philosophical Journal,* vol. 2 (1985), pp. 3-14.

4. Ilting 3, pp. 575, 578; cf. *HPR,* addition to §185, p. 267-8.

5. In Hegel's discussion of the legislature, Knox quite correctly translates *die Stände* or *das ständische Element* as 'the Estates'. In the section devoted to civil society, however, he translates *Stände* as 'classes' or 'social classes'. In my view, this translation is mistaken, largely because the term 'classes' is overlaid with specific and misleading twentieth-century connotations. This gives rise to two serious problems in interpretation. (i) Knox cannot make a distinction, in his English version of the *Philosophy of Right,* between *Stände* and *Klassen,* which is also translated as 'classes'. This completely misses the point that Hegel's social topography is three-dimensional. That is to say, he draws attention to 'vertical' divisions of wealth and power in society (*Klassen*) as well as 'horizontal' occupational divisions (*Stände*). (I am indebted to Allen Wood for this particular terminology.) (ii) The thrust of Hegel's crucial point that the Assembly of Estates (one of the institutions of state) is made up of the estates of civil society is lost on the reader of the English version. Hegel himself makes the point forcibly: 'Although in the view of so-called theories [of this kind] the estates of civil society and the Estates in their political significance [*die Stände in*

politischer Bedeutung] stand wide apart from each other, [the German] language has still maintained this unity which in any case they actually possessed in former times' (§303R). For these reasons, I render *Stand* as 'estate' throughout, reserving 'class' for *Klasse*. If the phrase 'the business estate', for example, sounds quaint and more old-fashioned than 'the business class', that is partly Hegel's point, and I try to capture it in my English version.

6. Ilting 3, p. 709; cf. *HPR*, addition to §255, p. 278; see also the cryptic reference to guilds (*Zünfte*) in Ilting 1 [the 1819 lectures], p. 323. As an example of the developments that Hegel was referring to, the political economist Turgot, during his tenure as Controller General of France, had issued an edict in 1776 to suppress the guilds, because they were obstructing the freedom of labour, and they were abolished completely in France in 1789. Corporations, however, were still being established in Great Britain and Ireland: in 1785, for example, an Act of Parliament established 'The Corporation for Preserving and Improving the Port and Harbour of Belfast'. See also G. Heiman, 'The sources and significance of Hegel's corporate doctrine', in Z.A. Pelczynski (ed.), *Hegel's Political Philosophy: Problems and Perspectives*, Cambridge University Press, 1971, pp. 111-35, which is very good on the sources, not so good on the significance. The author is quite wrong, for example, in claiming that Hegel's *Gewerbesstand* includes 'workers as well as managers'; but he is right to spell out the important differences between Hegel's 'corporatism' and 'the pseudo-corporatism of twentieth-century fascist Italy'. For a very brief account, which is derivative and rather unreliable in itself, but interesting because it locates Hegel's ideas within a historical sequence, see the chapter on Hegel's 'philosopy of the corporation', in Antony Black's *Guilds and Civil Society in European Political Thought from the Twelfth Century to the Present*, Methuen, London, 1983, pp. 202-9.

7. Ilting 3, p. 711; cf. *HPR*, addition to §255, p. 278; cf. Ilting 4, pp. 628-9, on 'the spirit of guilds [*der Zunftgeist*]' and freedom of business.

8. Hegel insists that 'it is only by being authorized that an association [*ein Gemeinsames*] becomes a corporation' (253R), but does not specify by whom it is to be authorized. By the executive?

9. Hegel blames the extremes of wealth and poverty in England on the abolition there of the corporations (by which, presumably, he means the guilds) (§245R). In his 1819/20 lecture course, Hegel is reported as drawing attention to 'the excesses of wealth and poverty from which England notoriously suffers. One can be sure

that one of the main causes of this is that the corporations do not exist there in an organic and systematic form. When each individual works only for himself, then the ethical element [*das sittliche Element*] is missing'. See *Philosophie des Rechts: Die Vorlesung von 18 19/20 in einer Nachschrift,* ed. D. Henrich, Suhrkamp, Frankfurt am Main, 1983, p. 207.

10. It is interesting to note that as a result of the civil rights campaign in Northern Ireland against religious discrimination in local government employment and services, since 1973 local services such as education, libraries, health and social services have been administered by public boards composed (unlike their counterparts elsewhere throughout the United Kingdom) of a mixture of elected local councillors and nominees appointed by government to represent various local interests such as voluntary community groups, employers' organizations, and trade unions. Many observers claim (and I agree with them) that this system has resulted in a much more equitable administration of these services than the one it replaced, which was controlled exclusively by elected local councillors.

11. I translate the phrase *das ständische Element* (and sometimes, when appropriate, *die Stände*) as 'Assembly of Estates'. It is quite clear from the context that Hegel is referring to 'the Estates element' of the legislature, but for some reason he almost never uses, in the published *Philosophy of Right,* the word *Ständeversammlung* (literally, Assembly of Estates), which he used habitually in all his lectures. He does write that '*die ständische Versammlung*' is divided into two chambers (§312); and he refers to 'the publicity of Assemblies of Estates [*Öffentlichkeit der Ständeversammlungen*]' (§319).

12. By *Privatstand* Hegel means **both** the agricultural and the business estates, i.e. those devoted essentially to private rather than public affairs. See Ilting 4, p. 709.

13. It is important to bear in mind that Hegel's 'agricultural estate' is made up of the aristocracy and the landed gentry; it does not include tenant farmers, peasants, farm labourers, and the like. See §§305-7 and §§312-13 for Hegel's argument for something very like the British House of Lords **before** the creation of life peers.

14. Knox systematically translates *die Abordnung* (and its variations) in terms of 'elections'. In fact, the term denotes simply the choice or appointment of deputies, with no specification as to how they are to be chosen or appointed. I think Knox's translation begs the interesting question.

15. It is sobering to reflect that in recent years 'the people' have elected to positions of great power Margaret Thatcher and Ronald Reagan. In Northern Ireland, 'democratic' elections have furthered the destructive aims of Ian Paisley and Gerry Adams ('with a ballot paper in one hand and an Armalite in the other'). It is also true to say that nowhere more than in Northern Ireland are elected politicians the prisoners of their own electorate, and any politician who seems to be making the slightest concession to 'the other side' is immediately cast aside.

16. Ilting 3, pp. 709-10; cf. *HPR*, addition to §255, p. 278.

17. Ilting 3, p. 710, cf. *HPR*, addition to §255, p. 278.

18. Knox translates Hegel's term *Meister* as 'master of his craft'. I am convinced that 'Meister' is just a direct translation by Hegel of the term 'master' used by Adam Smith and others to designate the employer in an industrial or agricultural enterprise. Smith, for example, habitually refers to the relationship between 'the master' and 'the workmen'. See, for example, Smith's discussion of 'the wages of labour' and industrial disputes, in *The Wealth of Nations* [1776], ed. W.B. Todd, 2 vols, Clarendon Press, Oxford, 1976, vol. I, 82-5. See also A. Ferguson, *An Essay on the History of Civil Society* [1767], ed. D. Forbes, Edinburgh University Press, 1966, p. 183.

19. Some reviewers of my *Hegel's Social and Political Thought*, Gill and Macmillan, Dublin and St. Martin's Press, New York, 1979 (including some who should have known better) betrayed a surprising refusal to acknowledge that Hegel had a thorough understanding of the vertical class division **within** the *Fabrikantenstand*, the manufacturing branch of the business estate. He reserved the term *Klasse* for the sub-groups within the *Fabrikantenstand*. To attempt to dismiss my earlier analysis of this particular question as 'ideological' (whatever that might mean) displays a pathetically blinkered reading of Hegel's own texts. He was referring to *'die arbeitende Klasse'* (i.e. the class of wage-earners) as early as 1803 (see his 'System der Sittlichkeit', in *Schriften zur Politik und Rechtsphilosophie*, ed. G. Lasson, Meiner, Leipzig, 1913, p. 498). He retains this usage throughout his career: in the published *Philosophy of Right* of 1820, he refers to 'the dependence and distress of the *Klasse* tied to that kind of [factory] work' (§243); he refers to the luxury and extravagance of the 'business classes [*der gewerbtreibenden Klassen*]' (§253R, see p. 27 above); he remarks that the burden of maintaining the poverty-stricken multitude (*Masse*) 'might be directly laid on the wealthier class [*der reichern Klasse*]' (§245). See also Ilting 3, p. 712. There should be no mystery about this. This kind of terminology had been a commonplace in the literature on political economy in the previous fifty years.

(For Smith's discussion of the conflicts between 'the masters' and 'the workmen', see the previous note.) Turgot, in a section of his *Reflections* [1766] headed 'Subdivision of the industrial stipendiary class into capitalist entrepreneurs and ordinary workmen', drew the distinction thus: 'The whole class which is engaged in meeting the different needs of society with the vast variety of industrial products [i.e. Hegel's *Fabrikantenstand*] finds itself, so to speak, subdivided into two orders: that of the entrepreneurs, manufacturers, and masters who are all possessors of large capitals which they turn to account by setting to work, through the medium of their advances, the second order, which consists of ordinary artisans who possess no property but their own hands, who advance nothing but their daily labour, and who receive no profit but their wages' (in *Turgot on Progress, Sociology and Economics*, ed. and trans. R.L. Meek, Cambridge University Press, 1973, p. 153). It is well established that Hegel was fully conversant with this literature: see, for example, §189R, where he cites Smith, Say, and Ricardo; cf. my *Hegel's Social and Political Thought*, pp. 70-72; cf. Paul Chamley, 'Les origines de la pensée économique de Hegel', *Hegel-Studien*, vol. 3 (1965), pp. 225-61. His whole discussion of civil society demonstrates his keen awareness of the socio-economic realities of early nineteenth-century capitalism. Just as an example, in 1823 he explained that as commerce (*der Handel*) thrives, 'the working class becomes more wretched and thus works for lower wages, so that the businessman can sell for a lower price [*je kümmerlicher die arbeitende Klasse ist und also wohlfeiler arbeitet, so daß der Kaufmann wohlfeiler verkaufen kann*]' (in Ilting 3, p. 712). When his wide and deep knowledge of political economy is allied to his ethical concerns, it comes as no surprise at all that he should declare (in 1825) that 'within society, penury [*der Mangel*] immediately takes the form of a wrong done to one class [*Klasse*] by another' (Ilting 4, p. 609; cf. *HPR*, addition to §244, pp. 277-8).

20. 'In considering the idea of the state [*bei der Idee des Staats*], we must not have our eyes on particular states or on particular institutions' (Ilting 4, p. 632; cf. *HPR*, addition to §258, p. 279).

21. Hegel was not nearly as harsh on 'the people' in his 1817/18 lectures in Heidelberg. Sée C. Becker et al. (eds), *Vorlesungen über Naturrecht und Staatswissenschaft* [the Wannenmann transcript], Meiner, Hamburg, 1983, especially pp. 219-21, 233-4. I am inclined to accept the view that Hegel had been frightened in the intervening period by the emergence of the so-called *Demagogenverfolgung* and the influence of his rabble-rousing colleague Fries (see his Preface, *HPR*, pp. 5-8).

22. Ilting 3, p. 801; cf. *HPR*, addition to §302, pp. 292-3.

23. Ilting 4, p. 692; cf. *HPR*, addition to §290, pp. 290-91.

24. While disagreeing with many of its details, I have every sympathy with Klaus Hartmann's project of developing a 'categorial social philosophy' taking its inspiration from Hegel, adumbrated in his essay, 'Towards a new systematic reading of Hegel's philosophy of right', in Z.A. Pelczynski (ed.), *The State and Civil Society: Studies in Hegel's Political Philosophy*, Cambridge University Press, 1984, pp. 114-36.

3 Ethics and the Hegelian State

ANDREW VINCENT

I Introduction

Is it reasonable to regard the state as an ethical institution embodying the true ends or purposes of individual citizens? Such a question today would meet with little sympathy or approval. The principle that the realm of the individual must be kept distinct from that of the state, except where an individual's action impedes another, is still firmly rooted in liberal-democratic thought. It is closely connected with the view that the public interest, if it exists, hardly ever coincides with the aggregate of individual interests in society. This is especially true in the realm of moral conduct. The function of law, as promulgated by the state, is not to enforce morality. Writers in the legal positivist tradition have, not without criticism, established this as an orthodoxy this century. However, such an idea would have sounded strange to Greek philosophers like Plato and Aristotle, and also to the medieval mind of St Thomas Aquinas.[1] They recognized that political institutions could either corrupt or sustain human beings, but at their best they could contribute to the perfection or salvation of individual citizens. Their function was primarily moral. In the Christian sense, as St Paul expressed it in Romans 13, government could represent the fatherly authority of God on earth. Such an idea became embodied in the patriarchal and divine right theories of the sixteenth century. The more contemporary grasp of the state as morally neutral is thus relatively novel in the European political vocabulary. The idea of moral neutrality has intellectual roots in the sixteenth century, specifically in thinkers like Hobbes. Hobbes discussed the state or commonwealth primarily in terms of centralizing power, security and sovereignty. Moral requirements, for the state and its ruler, came a poor second. Hobbes's thought contains the lineaments of the nineteenth- and twentieth-century emphasis on legal positivism and the separation of law and morality.

The most important perspective in nineteenth- and twentieth-century political thought which contributed to the separation of the realm of the individual from that of the state was 'liberal individualism'. It is admittedly a rather general category, yet very broadly the liberal individualist understands the political community as simply an area in which individuals can pursue their own self-chosen conceptions of the good life. The state acts as a neutral arbiter, which exists fundamentally to maintain a formal rule of law behind the flux and flow of individual actions. It does not exist to inculcate a moral outlook; that is the individual's concern. Moral education smacks of paternalism. Admittedly many liberals, including J.S. Mill, have not been averse to some paternalism, but it is something which must be carefully justified and used with caution.[2] The individual's liberty is sovereign. Ronald Dworkin summarizes this general conception when he states that liberal political theory

> supposes that political decisions must be, so far as possible, independent of any particular conception of the good life.... Since the citizens of a society differ in their conceptions, the government does not treat them as equals if it prefers one conception to another.[3]

In fact a number of recent political philosophers, like Dworkin, have addressed themselves to the nature of the relation of the state and the individual in liberal individualist terms. John Rawls and Robert Nozick, for example, go back to the traditional argument of justifying the state and political affairs from the ground upwards, namely, utilizing some kind of state of nature.[4] Nozick specifically is in direct intellectual descent from John Locke, although the social contract idea is excluded. The state comes about through a congeries of intentions. The 'invisible hand' of classical economics works silently in the background. The fallacy of the socialist argument, for the liberal individualist, is that because institutions are generated by human activity, the socialist thinks that by acting or intending collectively we can reshape institutions in line with our collective desire for the common good. The fallacy is that the outcome is hardly ever the intended consequence. Institutions are the unintended result of an aggregate of intentions. The resulting situation for Nozick is a minimal 'nightwatchman' state comparable to Herbert Spencer's 'committee of management'. The same theme is reflected in Hayek's work *Law, Legislation and Liberty*. Society and the state are, for Hayek, a catallactic order. Catallaxy implies a spontaneous order, rather than the deliberate pursuit of an end. The state is seen as the result, as in Nozick, of the 'invisible hand', constrained only by formal rules relating to property, tort and contract.[5]

The duty of the citizen is, therefore, not to deliberately pursue a common good, but rather to maintain a rule of law, a nomocratic order as opposed to a teleocratic one, in which individuals pursue their private goods. John Rawls also, although arriving at more interventionary and distributivist conclusions than Nozick or Hayek, still constructs his theory of justice on a classical economic model of man as a rational utility maximizer, with society regarded as a series of market relationships. Rawls does not see it as the state's function to define the moral goal of its citizens. The theory of justice posits some form of constitutional democracy, yet little is said about the authority which is to institute the proposals on justice. Where and how the principles of justice are to be applied is presumably left to the games theorists and moral strategists.

The liberal individualist understanding of the state has been strengthened by a number of points this century. First, the tradition of empirical political science has not encouraged normative questioning of the legitimacy of the state. The preoccupation with common-sense empirical inquiry has led to the investigation and comparison of the mechanics of the state rather than the attempt to articulate and criticize its normative content. Thus the liberal individualist understanding of the state is very much taken for granted. Second, the political scientist and the liberal individualist can appeal to the fact that the present state in Western industrialized societies is unfitted to be a moral educator. It is too large and impersonal, dominated by multifarious interests and factions, none of which has an exclusive claim to moral rectitude. Further, the climate of philosophy in Britain, specifically since the 1930s and 1940s, has tended to eschew the larger claims of traditional metaphysics. T.D. Weldon's *Vocabulary of Politics* typified the new form of rigorous, analytical and sceptical philosophy.[6] For Weldon the state was not the name of a thing. The intellectual pursuit of the state's essence was viewed as a distinctly unfruitful exercise. The analysis of language and concepts on a small scale led to a suspicion of the broader normative theory about the state. Finally, the only rigorous and politically effective alternatives to liberal individualism this century were socialism, specifically Marxist socialism, and anarchism. These latter traditions have been primarily concerned to unmask the state as a coercive institution. At best the state was a temporary aberration.

However, one distinctive point characteristic of the liberal individualist, anarchist, and Marxist traditions is that whether the state is seen as directly coercive, legal, democratic, or totalitarian, it is conceived of as standing over and against the citizen. It may be seen as necessary, but ultimately it is alien to the private interests and moral activity of the individual. The still widespread use of the term 'state interference' implicitly postulates a division between the state and the individual. The individual is understood, on this view, to be somehow constantly under threat from a state always ready to encroach upon individual liberty.

Yet such a conception of the state would not only sound strange to Greek and medieval thinkers but also to the more recent tradition stemming from Rousseau and continuing through Fichte, Hegel, Green, Bosanquet and Bradley. From Hegel specifically, the Idealist political tradition formulated a theory to overcome the one-sidedness of the liberal individualist theory of the relation of the state and the individual. For Idealists, the state should be viewed as a moral entity and moral educator. It was not something alien, or as the Idealists put it, 'other' than the individual's interests. However, since their arguments are predominantly concerned with metaphysics and the normative structure of the state, the Idealist account has not prospered this century. Also, the twentieth-century experience of fascism and totalitarianism has further associated Idealism with the Popperian 'closed society' and dampened intellectual interest.

My concern in this essay is to reconstruct the outline of the Idealist argument on the overcoming of the one-sidedness of liberal individualism, an outline which is not often adequately grasped. My major attention is given to Hegel and the relation between his metaphysics and politics; however, I do draw on sources in the British Hegelian tradition. I also review some of the major criticisms of the Idealist account. My contention is that the major weakness of the Idealist argument is not in its totalitarian or coercive possibilities. In fact, the most fruitful part of the Idealist account is its view of the state as embodying moral purposes. It provides the basis for a very positive theory of citizenship, which we have lost this century in the more negative views of liberal individualism. Rather, the principal weakness of the Idealist account lies in its inability to reconcile an intrinsic ethical egalitarianism, namely the demand that all citizens should equally be guaranteed the chance to develop their potentialities, with the existing inequalities and divisions of society in the nineteenth or twentieth century. This latter criticism is expanded in the last section of the paper.

II Radical Autonomy

The concept of the state in the Idealist tradition is complex compared with conventional liberal theories. This point can be illustrated in Hegel's usage. Hegel employs the word state in a number of senses. First, it refers to the body of codified laws, rules and procedures, which might be called the 'legalistic' definition of the state. This is recognizably a liberal individualist definition of the state, as outlined in the opening section. Also, it is a concept of the state which is reminiscent of the ideas of some twentieth-century legal positivists. However, Hegel also refers to the state in terms of the internal structure of a constitutional monarchy. Under this rubric the state is identified with the office of monarchy, the legislative and executive bodies. This is the state considered as an ideally organized government. This might be called the 'political' definition of the state. There is also the vaguely defined idea of the state in international politics, as a separate sovereign, national and geographical unit, defined against other sovereign national units. This might be called the 'internationalist' definition of the state. Finally, there is the most embracing sense of the state considered as a communal bond. In this sense, the state is a customary structure which embodies in its laws and institutions the real interests of its members. In this definition of the state, there is no discontinuity between the individual's will and the purposes embodied in the laws. This allows Hegel to claim that the truly subjective - the intrinsic desires and purposes of individual citizens - is rooted in the objective world of laws and institutions. This definition of the state, which may be called the 'ethical' definition, embraces the totality of persons and institutions. Thus all individuals and institutions, including the family, neighbourhood groups, classes, estates and so on, are all identified with the state. The state in this sense is neither a monolithic super-entity nor a governmental body. Rather it is a description of the whole structure of persons and institutions united by habitual communal rules. This is the sense of the state that I am primarily concerned with. In this case it could be somewhat misleading to speak of the 'state' and 'institutions', since in the ethical definition they are identified, although not merged.[7]

One of the distinctive characteristics of Hegel's philosophy of politics is that he is looking for a way of overcoming the alien quality of political and social institutions. One of the most important questions we are faced with in political philosophy is the relationship between the individual and the state. Hegel does not offer us any naive organicist or holistic theory to integrate these two elements; rather he tries to show, by an extremely subtle and occasionally bizarre argument, that the individual and the social world of institutions have essentially the same substance. This provides the answer to the problem of the alienation of individuals from institutions. Yet this 'substance' is not a simple identity; Hegel tries developmentally to show, through a complex analysis of the concept of the human mind, how mind presupposes the institutional structure of the social world. The work of the social theorist and philosopher are often kept distinct in contemporary thought; either the philosopher will investigate the concept of mind, or a sociologist will examine the nature of the social world. Hegel tries to combine the two lines of investigation, which is one of his great virtues. I would stress here that I am not concerned with elucidating the formal structure of institutions discussed by Hegel, which has been adequately covered by other Hegel scholars, but rather with the form of argument by which Hegel gets to the point of placing such value in institutions.

In order to construct this form of argument I will be primarily referring to the section on psychology in Hegel's *Philosophy of Mind*. This section is the last stage in the triadic structure of what

Hegel calls 'Subjective Spirit', which includes the previous sections on anthropology and phenomenology.

Hegel's concept of mind (*Geist*) does not fit very easily into any contemporary discussions of the philosophy of mind. This is primarily because he is not thinking of 'individual' minds. Individual minds are part of, or instances of, some kind of universal mind which is the essence of reality. This universal mind is embodied or immanent in the world, yet in individual minds it becomes conscious of itself and its own development. In this sense, the philosopher is an instance of the self-consciousness of this cosmic mind. The retrospective task of the philosopher is to apprehend the course of this development throughout the course of history.[8] As Hegel put it: 'Mind is ... in its every act only apprehending itself, and the aim of all genuine science is just this, that mind shall recognize itself in everything in heaven and on earth. An out-and-out Other simply does not exist for mind'.[9] The essential presupposition to grasp here is that reality is the development of this cosmic mind. This metaphysical presupposition immediately rules Hegel out of court for many contemporary philosophers. However, the difficulty is to know whether Hegel's thesis on this cosmic mind is to be taken theologically or anthropologically. Whereas some British Idealists, like T.H. Green, took Hegel theologically, neo-Hegelians like Feuerbach quite obviously took the latter position, which is slightly more acceptable to some contemporary philosophers.

The somewhat bizarre quality of this cosmic presupposition is only enhanced for contemporary commentators when we realize that this universal mind is 'self-creative'.[10] Mind is its own act. All categories are mind-dependent, including nature. The implication of this, put very crassly, is that when I say something is finite, it is mind in one of the stages of its development which has assumed the character of 'finiteness'. The individual presupposes limits. Yet when the individual realizes that he has presupposed this limit, he is on the way to overcoming it. To put this point in less abstruse terms; it is sometimes argued that the law always restricts freedom and limits the citizen. Therefore the less law, the greater freedom. This view is perfectly legitimate, at a certain stage, but it is constituted by the individual. It is mind which has posited law as a hindrance. The unselfconscious individual mind might assume that law must always restrict freedom in some way. Yet for the Hegelian it is a developmental stage of mind. Law does not have to be conceived of as a hindrance, since it is intrinsically 'mind-dependent'.

The Idealist proposition that mind is self-creative can be illustrated from the section on psychology in Hegel's *Philosophy of Mind*. Hegel works through three stages in the psychology section – Theoretical Mind, Practical Mind, and Free Mind. The latter stage is the high-water mark of the consideration of the individual subjective mind. All these stages are an attempt to elucidate the faculties of the human mind. Theoretical Mind deals with the development of the mind to the stage of 'formal thinking'. Hegel works through the stages of direct intuitive acquaintance – an unanalysed awareness similar to Kant's idea of *Anschauung* - through the development of imagination, recollection and memory, and finally to the stage of conceptual thought and judgement. Objects in the world are gradually taken up into the rational thought processes of the individual. The individual begins to possess the world intellectually in the form of conceptual knowledge. As Hegel puts it: 'What mind rationally knows, just because it is rationally known, becomes a rational content'.[11] The private intuitions that we possess, presumably at a younger age, are gradually transformed into a system of concepts and symbols. In thought, the individual grasps the world through a system of concepts. This analysis is a familiar type of enterprise that philosophers have always addressed themselves to, namely, the elucidation of faculties like intuition, memory, and thought; admittedly not many philosophers do it in this developmental mode. However, Hegel argues that the elucidation of these faculties in not enough. Thought can only grasp objects when it has **made** the objects fit its requirements. In other words, the individual does not passively observe the world but actually manipulates it. At this point Hegel begins the consideration of Practical Mind. For Hegel, the individual confronts a world which has already been manipulated by human praxis. In his perception of the world, the individual transforms it according to his likes, dislikes, impulses and motivations. It is at this juncture that Hegel comes to his account of human will. 'As will', Hegel argues, 'the mind is aware that it is the author of its own conclusions, the origin of its self-fulfilment'.[12] In the sphere of Practical Mind, the individual attempts to impress himself on the world, or to direct the world according to his interests. This is again very close to Kant's idea of *Willkür*, which refers to the arbitrary preference and choice of the individual.[13] The individual disciplines himself, controls his own impulses and chooses according to his capricious interests.

In a few deeply obscure paragraphs Hegel tries to show the dialectical mediation of Theoretical and Practical Mind into Free Mind.[14] Hegel's argument is based upon a radical distinction between mind and nature. In contemporary terminology, he is advancing an 'agency thesis'. Explanations of human activity are given in terms of the agent's reasons and intentions, not in terms of antecedent causes. In fact Hegel's thesis is one of 'radical autonomy'. Explanations cannot be given outside the agent. He has total responsibility for his actions. The actual transition to Free Mind seems to be a demonstration that thought implies practice and practice implies thought. Thus the practical transformation of the world implies that it has been intellectually and conceptually assimilated, but the intellectual and conceptual assimilation implies that the individual has transformed it. This is essentially the propositional structure of free will. Fully self-conscious free will is acquired when the agent can fully articulate and explain his own activity to himself and others. Free will is therefore attained when the individual realizes that he **is** radically autonomous. His thought and intentions are embodied in his actions. He can determine the content of his action. As Hegel puts it, Free Mind has infinite possibilities, 'because its object is itself and so is not in its eyes an "other" or barrier'.[15] The agent can abstract himself from anything.[16] The substance of thought is practice, practice is articulated in the will and the will implies freedom of choice.

For Hegel, free will is the solution to the problem of theory and practice. His argument is neatly summarized in the comment of the British Idealist T.H. Green, when he argued that in willing 'a man is his own object'.[17] Will is thought transferring itself into existence. This is the thesis of 'radical autonomy', which is reminiscent of Jean-Paul Sartre's existentialist theory of freedom. In Free Mind, the individual realizes his absolute radical autonomy.

III Will, Social Purpose and Positive Freedom

The thesis of radical autonomy is only the first step in the Idealist argument. The individual does not simply create his own content. He is not 'forced to be free'; and unlike Sartre's existentialist account, Hegel does not leave the individual with this 'intolerable freedom'. It is at this point that Hegel begins linking up his discussion of the concept of mind with his views on the social world. He tries to show that the faculties of the human mind, elucidated in the section on psychology, are integrally connected to certain forms of social order, and that certain types of order contribute to the development of these faculties. The method by which he demonstrates this is by restressing the fact that rationality is intersubjective and social in character.[18] In the final paragraphs of the section on Free Mind, Hegel argues that the individual becomes aware of his own creative capacity to determine his own actions. He controls his diverse desires and impulses, and structures them within his specific ends. For example, his specific end might be something perfectly harmless like fishing, or on the other hand it might be shooting people. However, one of the main problems with each individual pursuing a specific end is that it is socially unworkable.[19] If all individuals simply pursued their own specific ends, social and political confusion would prevail, unless one adhered to some kind of voluntaristic anarchism. Every person would be seeking a purely personal conception of happiness and the social world would be torn apart by individualistic caprice. Hegel is arguing here neither for total moral conformity, nor for the abandonment of harmless ends. However, he is arguing that there must be certain agreed normative ends upon which social life is based, for example, respect for each citizen's right to self-development. Concrete positive freedom exists when individuals control their impulses and desires through socially defined norms. Social norms should embody the recognition of others having similar claims to self-development. One must recognize others' rights to self-development in order for one's own claim to be recognized. This argument encapsulates the move towards a positive concept of freedom, which can be defined as self-creativity and self-determination within the parameters of social norms. As Hegel puts it: 'True liberty, in the shape of the moral life, consists in the will finding its purpose in a universal content, not in subjective or selfish interests'.[20] The subjective interests are not destroyed, but brought into the rule-governed framework of the social world. The arbitrary quality of the individual will is thus structured by what Hegel calls the concrete universal of social rules. Rationality is not something which the individual invents, rather it is derived from the social world as a rational practice.

Hegel therefore takes a traditional positive libertarian perspective, arguing that free will is dependent on the object willed. There must be a reconciliation between the 'objects of will', namely the individual interests, and the 'objects of reason', the social interests and norms. Freedom is the will determined by an object of reason. The objects of reason are derived from social institutions, like the family, neighbourhood association, corporation or estate and so on. 'By their existence', Hegel argues, 'the moral temper comes to be indwelling in the individual, so that in this sphere of particular existence ... he is **actually** free'.[21] Hegel calls these institutions which are imbued with reason 'Objective Mind'. This truly free will was often described in the British Idealist tradition as the common will or common good.

The transition from 'a free will' to the 'common will' or from 'a mind' to the 'social mind' has often worried specifically Anglo-Saxon commentators. The same problem arises in the synonymity between the individual's good and the common good. A number of points need to be made here. The Idealist argument is not nearly so alarming as it is sometimes made out to be. First, the adjective 'common' implies 'that which is shared or characteristic of a group'. Individuals in a community participate in common institutions, like the family or educational structure. In this mundane sense they share institutions and the norms characteristic of them. For Hegel, norms embody social purpose and therefore human will. Therefore, the individuals who participate in these institutions share a common will. Since institutions ought to embody the means of making citizens free and ethical, they encapsulate a will common to all. In growing within such institutions the individual assimilates the common norms and in so doing develops the characteristics of free will. Institutions, as the result of human praxis, embody substantively the same content as individual minds. They embody past and present generations of thought and purpose. The Idealists therefore thought that institutions were externalized concepts, literally social mind, or as Hegel called them 'Objective Mind'. This argument is advancing, in a somewhat convoluted form, a socialization thesis. Thus to try to draw the individual distinct from the social world is to engage in what the Idealists called hopeless abstraction. In fact the Idealist argument is a very traditional one deriving from Greek political theory, specifically Aristotle, where the identification and understanding of the rational autonomous individual entails a close study of the rule-governed framework of the social world of institutions.

IV Institutions and the Will

Thus the Idealist argument is that the individual determines himself autonomously, yet this subjective freedom is socially unworkable. Freedom, properly understood, must be consonant with the development of the person. Pure licence or even simple 'opportunities to act' tells us very little about such development. The opportunity, ability or desire to engage in mass murder does not provide a particularly enlightening elucidation of freedom. For Hegel, freedom is concerned with increasing self-control over one's diverse impulses and motivations and consequently accepting norms which further this end. It is also concerned with accepting norms which contribute towards the equal development of all persons in religious, moral, aesthetic and philosophical fields. The end of political association for Hegel, following directly upon Aristotle, is the attainment of the highest forms of human excellence and virtue. This could not possibly be achieved in a situation of rampant individualism and licence. Respect for and recognition of other persons is an essential prerequisite of freedom. Institutions which embody this principle of respect and which cultivate the equal development of persons (*Bildung*) are therefore consonant with freedom. The rule-governed framework of such institutions is based upon the ideal of self-development and freedom. The fully-rounded, harmonious individual is one who has disciplined his own subjective impulses through common public rules, which embody an unconditional commitment to the equal development of all citizens. The philosophy of institutions is therefore designed to show their implicit teleology. Human praxis has established the institutions, yet the rules form the substance of rational human praxis. The elusive quality of this argument is to know whether an individual's freedom and good is simply to follow a formal rule of respect for others, or whether it is something more substantial, namely following certain cultural goals. The former point makes freedom and goodness rather too formal and general in character. The latter creates a somewhat relativistic picture, where each individual will be pursuing his own culturally defined goal. One answer to this problem lies in Hegel's idea of the 'concrete universal'. The formal rule of respect is situated in the established customs of the community which themselves encourage the self-development of the individual through culturally defined goals. The problem still remains as to whether the idea of the concrete universal is simply a verbal sleight of hand.

Apart from the elusiveness of this argument, the more common objection at this point is that freedom is being identified with a higher rational self; also, whatever is free corresponds to the higher self and is therefore necessarily good. This claim, for many critics, leads to unacceptable moral and political absolutism or totalitarianism. Someone will be defining what constitutes the higher rational self and therefore will decide in what manner people can be free or forced to be free. The argument continues that the Idealist makes nonsense of words like freedom and good, since it would be impossible to speak of worthless or criminal 'free' actions. Some critics would also add to this point that the Idealist account of freedom does not correspond to the meaning of freedom in ordinary language.[22] This latter point has little critical worth since the Judaeo-Christian tradition of thought, which embodies positive libertarian ideas, has always been a part of ordinary language. The Pauline idea of 'freedom in the spirit' is a typical example of this. Further, much of the time ordinary language reflects confused and half-baked theories and consequently needs to be critically understood. The idea of the higher rational self is a strange misconception. It is difficult to identify any precise passages in Hegel where such terminology occurs. One big impasse here is that Idealism has a very different metaphysical understanding of the self from contemporary philosophy and liberal individualism. It is difficult not to see much of this discussion of the 'higher self' as indicative of a deeper-rooted metaphysical confrontation. However, all the Idealists seem to be arguing is that freedom is initially about the increasing observation and control of unreflective impulses by the individual, that is to say learning to be a self-conscious agent. This involves, ultimately, the acknowledgement of others as agents in their own right. Thus freedom involves the attempt to look at others' needs and interests on a broader and more comprehensive level. This particular argument does not deny that an individual could ignore others and perform a worthless action. The action would be free, but in a less adequate, comprehensive or rational sense. It would also be less good, since it did not acknowledge the equal right of all to self-development and freedom.

Admittedly, some of the Idealist claims do sound extremely odd. For example, institutions are viewed analogously to the individual will. They are practices unified and made coherent by social purpose. The key distinction to the individual will is that institutions, like the family, are underpinned by a complex tradition and are therefore seen as more certain and continuous than the transitory and irregular nature of the individual will. This idea led the British Idealist, J.H. Muirhead, to remark:

> Institutions are not men. On the other hand living institutions ... represent the past efforts and present cooperation of many individuals directed to a single and continuous purpose, and in this account may claim an individuality of their own.[23]

He goes on to characterize institutions as 'objectified purpose', which is essentially the same as Hegel's idea of 'Objective Mind'. This particular line of argument gives rise to some serious problems, which can be marshalled along the following lines: (1) institutions seem to be considered as more important than individuals; (2) surely empirical institutions have never lived up to the Idealist claims; inevitably they are dominated by elites or factions who will define the social norms; (3) if (1) and (2) are the case, how could the individual criticize institutions, since they would define his real interests. The route seems to be open once again for some form of tyranny.

The Idealist answers to these questions are based upon the implicit teleology of institutions which are viewed instrumentally, in the sense that they are unconditionally directed at the self-development of all individuals in the society. Although the individual comes into a world of given meanings and rules, nonetheless these rules are the result of reflective human agency. The social world is organized to afford the conditions for the development of agents.[24] By maturing within institutions the individual rises from pupillage to critical participation. This creates a double function in institutional life and overcomes the potential charge of conservatism, since individuals do not simply accept the status quo, but also actually criticize it. When the individual is mature and self-reflective, he can then apply his powers to criticize the institutions to make them more adequate embodiments of ethical purpose.[25] The fundamental norms sustain and are sustained by individual critical praxis. The test of an institution's worth is its ability to provide the conditions for self-development. It is perfectly possible to have bad or inadequate states.[26] These may be ruled by élites which rely on tyranny or slavery, but for the Idealists there are critical standards to apply to such states. However, one must always remember that Hegel's vision of the state was that of a very moderate constitutional monarchy, with a complex pluralistic structure of mediating groups within society. The British Idealists in turn accepted the existing Parliamentary structure as perfectly adequate.

Where these criticisms of Idealism might be said to gain some purchase is on the distinction between the ideal and the empirical state. The argument maintains that the Idealist attitudes on the state work at a purely prescriptive and ideal level. The whole structure of argument is simply an 'ought-to-be'. Unfortunately, in the real world, states do not function as ideal units. The only answer that the Idealists can give to this is to say that their argument is an elaboration of the real teleology of the state. Therefore, empirical states are imperfect manifestations of the real state. This is certainly one reading that can be given of Hegel; however, many would find this a deeply mystical and unsatisfactory notion which cannot really be grasped outside the metaphysical premises of Hegelian and Platonic essentialism. This line of thought has led many critics to argue that ultimately Idealists only overcame the otherness and alienation of the political and social world in their heads. The real world remained imperfect and impervious. It is at this point that Marx begins his criticism of Hegel.[27] Paradoxically, with hindsight, we can see Marx's implicit Idealism. Communism, like the Hegelian state, has remained in the domain of ideality and as yet has not showed itself as the implicit teleology of actual societies. Despite this point, sense can be made of the distinction between the real and ideal in the context of Idealist claims about the possibilities of human nature. Human nature is seen as a developing process.

Political institutions exist to further this process. The ideal institutions are those which embody this norm. The real problem arises on the question as to whether the theorist can accept the metaphysical assumptions about human nature and the role of social life. For Idealists, like Hegel, the real cannot be understood independently from the ideal. As argued earlier, for Hegel, mind is its own act.

To summarize briefly the Idealist argument; institutions are customary modes of behaviour which embody fundamental norms and concrete forms of morality. They provide the ground for the equal ethical cultivation of all individuals. The individual acquires the most fundamental norms by participating in social life, since social life expresses the ontological structure of human nature. To deny one's citizenship, for many Idealists, is in essence to deny one's humanity. The state, in the most complex 'ethical' sense, embodies the structure of will. As Hegel put it:

> The basis of right is, in general, mind; its precise place and point of origin is the will. The will is free, so that ... the system of right is the realm of freedom made actual, the world of mind brought forth out of itself like a second nature.[28]

Salvation, theologically and secularly, lies in a deeper understanding of this world and not another. It is no wonder that the British Idealist, Bernard Bosanquet, should have written a paper with perfect philosophical sincerity, entitled 'The Kingdom of God on Earth'. As he states in the paper: 'All we mean by the kingdom of god on earth is the society of human beings who have a common life and are working for the common social good'.[29] It was in this light that the Idealists viewed the state with its constitutive institutions as embodying will and purpose. Thus it is my contention that Hegel and the Idealist tradition provide sound arguments for an ethical egalitarianism. They also provide the basis for a positive concept of citizenship. Whether this ethical egalitarianism is consistently borne out in practice is a point that I wish to address in the final section.

V Otherness Overcome?

The preceding sections of this essay reveal a comprehensive theory of political obligation, as well as a criterion for evaluating institutions. The theory, in sum, is that institutions embody social purpose, which forms the substantive character of the citizen's will. The criterion for evaluating institutions would be whether they substantively embodied social purpose, the constitutive factor of human will. The theory articulated is summarized in T.H. Green's remark that 'To ask why I am to submit to the power of the state, is to ask why I am to allow my life to be regulated by that complex of institutions without

which I literally should not have a life to call my own'.[30] The
Idealist theory is very close to some recent conceptual arguments on
obligation, namely those which claim that to understand semantically
the concept of the state is to grasp one's obligations. It is therefore
no use asking further questions about why I ought to obey. For the
Idealists and some recent analytical theorists the concept of the
state implies obligation and 'ought'.[31]

Yet despite the Idealist argument on overcoming the otherness of
institutions like the state, there is something odd if we reflect on
Hegel's formulation of the state in the context of civil society in the
Philosophy of Right. Embodied in the theory of civil society is
another distinctive account of obligation. This is the contractual
theory of obligation. It must be remembered that Hegel's discussion
of civil society involves the description of a basically free market
society. Hegel's intellectual sources for this description lie in the
Scottish school of classical political economy, specifically Adam
Smith and Adam Ferguson. This notion of civil society embodies
many of the ideas of liberal individualism. For Hegel, this
participation in the market was a necessary moment in human
development. The individual cannot leap over this stage. The kind of
assumptions that we traditionally find in this position are that the
individual is naturally free, that he gives up this freedom only by
voluntary consent and contract, and that this contract protects
individuals from the otherness of the state. This state serves the
interests of the individual consenters. Neither Hegel nor the Idealist
tradition was at home in this position; both criticized it extensively
and posited its supersession. But the puzzling question remains, how
is this to be done? Now this question would seem to be answered in
the body of this essay, but there remain some more queries to be
answered.

Presumably, as civil society and individualism are necessary
components of the state and human development, there must always
be a large proportion of the population who are committed to civil
society, the domain of the understanding and individualism. In fact,
since this is the wealth producing element, it is a practical necessity
for it to be present in any state. If this is so, then a large proportion
of the population in business, agriculture and industry must be
committed to the view of the state as 'otherness' and contract.
These sizeable groups could not adopt views other than this, since
they would not otherwise have the cognitive perspective to engage in
civil society. Apart from these groups, we have the 'throw-offs'
from the process of civil society, the poor and unemployed. The
'pauperized rabble' in Hegel, or the 'denizen of the London yard' for
T.H. Green, hardly attain freedom in the Hegelian state.[32] As has
been discussed recently, poverty is not adequately reconciled within
the Hegelian system.[33] Presumably the view of the poor on
obligation cannot be contractual. They have no property to protect,
and they have not consented to authority, except tacitly. So their
view of the state must be as a force or power. They are obligated
only because they are forced to obey. The state may be paternalistic

or charitable, but it is completely 'other' or alien to them. Only the educated and developed rationality views the state as an ethical idea. The educated do not need to worry themselves with theories of obligation. They know that their wills are embodied in and constitutive of the state, without which they would not have a life to call their own.

Therefore we find here three distinctive accounts of obligation: the obligation based on force, the obligation generated by consent and contract, and finally the obligation generated by the rational will embodied in institutions. Now this might be seen as a developmental sequence but for one fact. These accounts represent more or less fixed groups in society and consequent conceptions of obligation. Does Hegel envisage that those who have acquired ethical consciousness will descend to the market place or cave with an individualistic mentality? Is it even possible to move fluidly up and down the Hegelian system? So what does happen to the pauperized rabble, the denizen of the London yard and the general working population? Hegel obviously implied that developmental growth to freedom was imminent, yet for whom? Unless one speculated about successive reincarnations, it is difficult to see how any of these groups could achieve any realization of the ethical life.

To be fair to Hegel, he did not mean these groups to be totally excluded. It is obvious that most individuals are born into families. Therefore, for Hegel, they participate in the first ethical root of the state. The ethical life of the family, which transforms natural desire into ethical service and natural acquisitiveness into family property, provides the unconscious elements of ethical life.[34] Ethical consciousness is acquired rudimentarily in the form of natural feelings. In schools, if the child is not too poor to go, he follows the abstract path of spirit through the academic disciplines.[35] He thus acquires some theoretical knowledge of ethical life. In society he continues his education through participation in the corporation, neighbourhood or his own profession. But what if he remains a shopkeeper, industrial worker or unemployed pauper? Presumably the ethical view of the state remains sublimated, an 'ought to be'. It is seen only as an abstraction and thus inadequate to express the condition of the agent's mind. The state remains alien and 'other' and is not overcome. Therefore, despite the interest of the Idealists' argument, there is considerable ambiguity as to whom it applies to. Perhaps one of the solutions to this problem is to take a leaf out of the book of the British Idealists earlier this century, namely, to encourage all, employers and workforce, to read Hegel and Idealist philosophy. But the question remains, what would they be or do afterwards? Thus Hegel and the Idealist tradition do not adequately reconcile the existing inequalities and divisions of capitalist free market society with the radical ethical egalitarianism proposed in the metaphysics. The Idealist concept of the state is therefore caught on the horns of a dilemma.

Notes

1. I am not suggesting that either Plato, Aristotle or Aquinas had a concept of 'the state' as such, since it did not appear in the European political vocabulary till approximately the sixteenth century.

2. On Mill's paternalism, see C.L. Ten, *Mill on Liberty*, Clarendon Press, Oxford, 1980, Chapter 7.

3. Ronald Dworkin, 'Liberalism', in Stuart Hampshire (ed.), *Public and Private Morality*, Cambridge University Press, 1980.

4. See Robert Nozick, *Anarchy, State and Utopia*, Basic Books, New York, 1974; John Rawls, A *Theory of Justice*, Oxford University Press, 1972.

5. See F.A. Hayek, *Law, Legislation and Liberty*, vol. II, *The Mirage of Social Justice*, Routledge and Kegan Paul, London, 1976, Chapter 10, pp. 107-132.

6. T.D. Weldon, *The Vocabulary of Politics*, Penguin, Harmondsworth, 1953.

7. For a clear discussion of the complexity of Hegel's idea of the state, see Z.A. Pelczynski, 'The Hegelian conception of the state', in *Hegel's Political Philosophy: Problems and Perspectives*, edited by Z.A. Pelczynski, Cambridge University Press, 1971, pp. 1-29.

8. This refers to the well-known description of the role of the philosopher, in the Preface to the *Philosophy of Right, HPR*, pp. 12-13.

9. *HPM*, §377, Zusatz, p. 1.

10. *HPM*, §§441 and 442.

11. *HPM*, §445, Zusatz, p. 191.

12. *HPM*, §469, p. 228.

13. See Lewis White Beck, A *Commentary on Kant's Critique of Practical Reason*, The University of Chicago Press, 1960, pp. 176-181.

14. *HPM*, §§479 and 480.

15. *HPR*, §22, p. 30. As Hegel grandiosely comments in the *Philosophy of Mind*, mind 'is confident that in the world it will find its own self, that the world must be reconciled with it, that, just as Adam said of Eve that she was flesh of his flesh, so mind has to seek in the world Reason that is its own Reason', §440, Zusatz, pp. 179-180.

16. See *HPR*, §5, p. 21.

17. T.H. Green, *Lectures on the Principles of Political Obligation*, Longmans, London, 1941, p. 2.

18. 'Restressing' in the sense that he has argued this point in the phenomenology section of the *Philosophy of Mind*.

19. Hegel gives a detailed dialectical reading of the transition from Free Mind to Objective Mind. This sentence gives a rather crude personal interpretation of the major upshot of Hegel's arguments on the transition. He does not think that individualism *per se* is unworkable, but rather 'atomic individualism'. Hegel is thinking of an ethical definition of the individual as adequate to Objective Mind.

20. *HPM*, §469, p. 228.

21. *HPM*, §482, p. 240. For a similar statement of this argument, see T.H. Green, *Lectures*, p. 15.

22. See W.L. Weinstein, 'The Concept of Liberty in Nineteenth-Century English Political Thought', *Political Studies*, vol. 13 (1965). For a broader claim, see I. Berlin, 'Two Concepts of Liberty', in his *Four Essays on Liberty*, Oxford University Press, 1967.

23. J.H. Muirhead (ed.), *Birmingham Institutions*, Cornish Brothers, Birmingham, 1911, p. vii. See also J.H. Muirhead and H.G.W. Hetherington, *Social Purpose: A Contribution to a Philosophy of Civic Society*, George Allen and Unwin, London, 1918, p. 122.

24. This is one of the most well-known lines of argument in the British Idealist tradition; see J.H. Muirhead, *Reflections by a Journeyman in Philosophy on the Movement of Thought and Practice in his Time*, George Allen and Unwin, London, 1942, pp. 160-1.

25. As Charles Taylor has remarked, 'practices and institutions are maintained only by ongoing activity, and must be, for it is only the ongoing practice which defines what the norm is our future action must seek to sustain', *Hegel and Modern Society*, Cambridge University Press, 1979, p. 89.

26. The bad state, according to Hegel, has no 'genuine actuality', *HPR,* addition to §270, p. 283; see also addition to §258, p. 279. A typically bad state would be one based upon slavery, which did not acknowledge the right to freedom and self-development. Hegel describes slavery as an 'outrage on the conception of man', *HPR,* §2, p. 15.

27. See S. Hook, *From Hegel to Marx,* University of Michigan Press, Ann Arbor, 1968.

28. *HPR,* §4, p. 20.

29. Bernard Bosanquet, 'The Kingdom of God on Earth', in Bosanquet, *Science and Philosophy and Other Essays,* George Allen and Unwin, London, 1927, p. 344.

30. Green, *Lectures,* p. 122.

31. T.D. Weldon, *Vocabulary of Politics,* Penguin, Harmondsworth, 1953, pp. 56-7; T. McPherson, *Political Obligation,* Routledge and Kegan Paul, London, 1967; H. Pitkin, 'Obligation and Consent', in P. Laslett, W.G. Runciman, and Q. Skinner (eds), *Philosophy, Politics and Society,* series four, Blackwell, Oxford, 1972, p. 77. For analysis and counterblast, see C. Pateman, *The Problem of Political Obligation,* Wiley and Sons, 1979. There is a strong similarity between the Idealists' argument that institutions and conventions are structured and help structure mind and the more contemporary argument that language and meaning are social practices governed by rules. As R.J. Bernstein has argued, 'One of the most dominant themes in analytic philosophy has been that language and human action are rooted in intersubjective practices and forms of life', *The Restructuring of Social and Political Theory,* Methuen, London, 1979, p. 230. The general theme is that language is socially dependent. It is rooted in customary behaviour, social practices, or forms of life. A child grows up in a world of given meanings. He or she does not learn language through picking up isolated words, but rather assimilates the meaning of words through complex verbal contexts. Concepts are learnt through their public uses. This provides the possibility for intersubjective meanings, since the ways in which we experience the world and social life are expressed in terms of publicly available concepts. Intersubjectivity provides common meanings and referents, the possibility of a common understanding and grasp of norms.

32. Green, *Lectures,* p. 8; *HPR,* addition to §240, p. 277.

33. Cf. Raymond Plant, 'Hegel and Political Economy', *New Left Review*, nos. 103 and 104 (1977); Bernard Cullen, *Hegel's Social and Political Thought*, Gill and Macmillan, Dublin, and St. Martin's Press, New York, 1979, pp. 85-91.

34. Cf. *HPR*, §175, p. 117.

35. Cf. *PS*, §28, p. 16.

4 Hegel and Economic Science

GEOFFREY HUNT

Economic theory in its dominant trends is in crisis, unable as it is to make sense of the current global crisis in the real economic world. It might seem unlikely that the philosophy of G.W.F. Hegel could play an important role in the remoulding of a science of economics. But I believe that there is still something living and useful in Hegel's philosophy, as long as we know how to extract it. It provides us with a uniquely concatenated set of categories which can coherently and suggestively order our theorizing about objects and events which are at once subjects and actions.[1] There are at least two ways in which a Hegelian contribution to economic science may be understood: (1) in terms of a development of the economics contained within the Hegelian philosophical system; (2) in terms of a recasting of Hegel's self-determining categorial structure, presented in his *Logic,* as an open-ended methodology for social science. I shall argue that the first is obstructive to the elaboration of an economic science appropriate to the present age, while the second is necessary to this elaboration. As a means of making my case I shall criticize Richard Dien Winfield's recent attempt to revive Hegelian political economy.[2]

I Extracting the Rational Kernel

The main philosophical obstacle to a Hegelian reassessment of mainstream economics, which is largely another way of speaking of one major obstacle presented to understanding Marx's theory and its possible extensions, is the question of the **possibility** of extracting a methodology from Hegel's system, an extraction which Hegelians would disallow, and Marxists have failed to adequately explain.[3]

Winfield emphasizes Hegel's philosophy as a project which circumvents the problems of traditional philosophies which **presuppose** the givenness of reality (what I shall call the ontological presupposition problem) or presuppose the correspondence of thought and reality rather than proving their correspondence (the epistemological presupposition problem).[4] I do not disagree with Winfield's main line of interpretation of Hegel, and now briefly give my own understanding of that interpretation.

Hegel's project succeeds, apparently, because he makes reality and thought self-grounding or, what is the same thing, foundationless. Thought is not grounded on experienced reality (empiricism) nor is it merely 'given' (rationalism, transcendental idealism) but is self-grounded. Reality is not grounded on thought (idealism) nor is it a 'given' (realism) but is also self-grounded. The self-groundedness is shown by deriving them both from a single pre-ontological, pre-epistemological (or post-ontological, post-epistemological) source in such a way that one **is** the other, but in a different form from the other. There is an essential identity in an apparent difference. This source is the categorial structure explicated (or self-explicated) in the *Logic*.[5] To find this convincing one would first have to accept the adequacy of Hegel's transition from the Absolute Idea, which terminates the *Logic,* to Nature (initially, Space and Time) which begins the ontological and epistemological movement from the Philosophy of Nature through the Philosophy of Spirit. I call this the 'second strategic transition'. Also, one would have to accept Hegel's account of how this pre-ontological and pre-epistemological realm is itself presented as a necessity and not an arbitrary starting point. In other words, one would have to accept Hegel's transition from Absolute Knowledge, which terminates the Philosophy of Spirit, to the *Logic* (initially, Being). This I call the 'first strategic transition'.

Hegel thus has a special kind of circular argument in which thought and reality issue from the *Logic,* and the *Logic* is shown to be a necessary consequent of the inadequacies of the thought-reality relation. The argument is a self-determining one. Wherever one starts in the circle the logic of one's location pushes one on to the next position, and so on around the circle. An extremely ingenious and quite unique solution to a host of perennial philosophical problems. So the key to Hegelian 'science' is that all the logical categories are self-generated from the initial category, Being, **before** the question of reality and its nature (its content) is even posed. As reality is presented, at the end of the *Logic* and the beginning of the Philosophy of Nature, as the self-externalization of the Absolute Idea, reality and thought emerge in the mould of the categorial structure of which they are both dimensions, reality being the phenomenal form of the Idea.

In the light of all this I think one can see without much difficulty why Hegelians say that one cannot extract a methodology from Hegel's system without making nonsense of both the system and the method: both the system and the method lose their point when they are separated. So my task is to show that an extraction can be made, admittedly at the expense of Hegel's system, in such a way as to satisfy any concerns we may have about dealing satisfactorily with the presupposition problems. I assume here that Hegel's two strategic transitions taken in themselves are logically sound or could be made so. The real question is the character of what one is left with after the transitions have taken place, and it is the second strategic transition, from *Logic* to Nature, which concerns me more.

Hegelians would have it, presumably, that the extraction of the self-determining categorial structure of the *Logic* out of the context of Hegel's system in order to 'apply' that structure to a 'given subject matter' reproduces the very problems Hegel had tried to overcome.[6] For now questions would arise again of assuming the nature of reality and of how we can justify our methodology or how we can be sure it is not a merely arbitrary construction (because we have now jettisoned the first strategic transition); and of how we could know that the methodology corresponds to or fits reality (because we have jettisoned the second strategic transition). As for the self-determining character of the categorial structure, this does not appear to be at issue, for it need not in itself be affected by the extraction, for we now simply take Being as a starting point in a special way, which I shall explain later.

It is not, then, really a question of whether we **can** extract the categorial structure, but of whether having extracted it it still has any merit. The first merit, which I shall illustrate later, is that it provides us with a rich internally related set of categorial determinations which is a great advance on the usual mono-categorial structures (e.g. Ancient Philosophy's 'forms', or mechanism's 'causes') and on fragmentary, syncretic structures. The second merit flows not from the categorial structure as such but from the manner in which it may be newly understood, that is, the place that may be found for it in an open-ended approach to science. My point is that although the extraction of this structure from Hegel's system **does** entail the epistemological presupposition problem this consequence is not so much a 'problem' as a necessary condition of science itself.

My argument for an understanding of Hegel's categorial structure, detached from his system and implanted in another open-ended approach which endorses the epistemological presupposition 'problem' is the other side of an argument for the inadequacy of Hegel's system as a **science.** I now briefly present this dual argument.

Basically, Hegel solves the epistemological presupposition problem by first solving the ontological one, and that by means of a self-referential device at the end of the *Logic* (the second strategic transition). Hegel's argument, so far as I understand it, is that in completing the process of self-determination the Idea is **both** the complete **unity** of all its determinations **and** those determinations themselves. This completion is in this way at once an externalization. The Idea is now, as unity, something other than the process of its coming to completion. It is form, and it is the form of its own content. Being is no longer abstract but 'full' of concrete determinations - it is real, it is nature. That is, being repeats itself but in external form. Hegel is careful to point out that this is not a 'transition' on the same level as the previous ones in the movement from being to Absolute Idea - it is a 'liberation' (what I have been calling a **strategic** transition'). He says:

> the pure Idea in which the determinateness or reality of the Notion is itself raised into Notion, is an absolute **liberation** for which there is no longer any immediate determination that is not equally **posited** and itself Notion.[7]

The determinateness of Notion is itself raised to a Notion, a Notion that abides with itself, a Notion of the Notion.

The fundamental point I wish to make about this self-externalization of the Idea is that it is not at all what Hegel takes it to be. The *Logic* does not, after all, unfold a pre-ontological and pre-epistemological realm (whatever that could be) but the **thought** of such a realm, Hegel's thought. This is as devastating a point for Hegel's philosophical claims as it is utterly trite. Tne self-referent of any thought can only be another thought. The self-referent of the thought of a pre-ontological realm may be designated the **thought** of reality, but it is not reality. Now it is quite easy to see how the thought of reality has the kind of relation to thought in general (and to methodology) which Hegel claims for reality itself. It is easy to see how the thought of reality can be made to unite with thought, although what results is, once again, not a pre-ontological realm but the thought of such a realm, the thought of a thought-reality unity. Hegel solves the ontological presupposition problem with an unrecognized presupposition of his own, namely that reality is the thought of reality, that practice is the thought of practice.[8] The consequence of this is that his self-referential device only solves the presupposition problems by **excluding** all possibility of genuine open-ended experiential content. Although for Hegel the Idea is supposed to generate its own content, the only content which can be generated from any thought by self-reference, whatever that thought is, is another thought. Admittedly, Hegel's 'reality' is distinguishable from his Idea, but only in the way, to give an analogy, that 3 is distinguishable from 3^2; they are both numbers even if the second is the first raised to a second power.

Hegel could only take the idea of reality for reality itself because he took the idea of a pre-ontological realm as a pre-ontological realm or, to put it differently, because he suspended the **extra**-conceptual conditions of his conceiving anything. The philosopher **as** philosopher taking flight in 'this pure ether as such'[9] puts aside as irrelevant the churnings of his stomach together with the rest of the real world until the world rudely interrupts the flight with a call for lunch. Thus Hegel's problematic (the presupposition problem) is misconceived, for practice and reality is already a presupposition, an inescapable one. Hegel only succeeds in making the **thought** of reality disappear in Absolute Knowledge while the reality which is not necessarily in anyone's thought at all stubbornly continues on its way.

If it is said that the foregoing remark is question-begging, this is absolutely true. I am assuming what supposedly should be demonstrated philosophically and what the history of philosophy shows cannot be demonstrated philosophically, namely that there is a given reality. Hegel takes the only path left to a purely philosophical approach with an ingenious self-referential device. But he has one thing in common with the failed philosophers before him - he assumes that the question of the givenness of reality is a question which **thought** can resolve. The fact that the thought which resolves it, for Hegel, is a tacit thought about non-thought and non-reality (Logic) makes no difference whatsoever. Reality cannot be derived from thought, including thought about non-thought, even if the thought of reality can. In short, the ontological presupposition problem is a pseudo-problem, for the very posing of the problem presupposes reality, indeed a problem-posing reality. Where there is no reality no problems whatsoever, including problems about the existence of reality, can be posed.

That the specific **character** of reality should not be presupposed is another matter, an epistemological one. The problem now is the correspondence of thought and reality and how to avoid the pitfalls of empiricism, rationalism and transcendental idealism. I shall approach this in rather a different way. What if instead of taking the categorial structure as the pre-ontological realm from which reality/thought issues we take self-developing reality, or more specifically an epochal set of social practices, as the realm from which thought issues, including the most general level of thought? This again looks question-begging: how can we characterize a set of social practices independently of thought and categories? And however we do characterize it how can we know that the characterization is not arbitrary, etc.? I wish to suggest a realist approach which both accepts this question-begging characteristic as necessary and as contingent depending on one's historical location. This realist philosophy need not pose the traditionally **static** and abstract problem of how we justify the methodology if, reinterpreting a lesson of Hegel, it can be shown **at a certain historical point** that the methodology is not arbitrary in a given social formation but the necessary reflection in thought of the most general features of the phenomenal structure of the society in which it arises. The categorial structure is well-founded and works because it repeats in forms of thought general features of the society.[10]

In other words, it **is** a question of presupposing a correspondence one cannot justify, but only at the epochal time the methodology in question is wholly appropriate. At that time it cannot, of necessity, be justified. When society has self-developed to a point which demands new forms in thought then and only then can the correspondence be **seen** for what it is, a reflection in thought of certain features of a social formation. Then it **can** be justified, and is always found wanting. Thus the paradox that a categorial structure can only be grounded in thought when its grounding is rejected. When it is grounded it cannot be grounded in thought, and when it can be grounded in thought then it is no longer grounded. To give an example, when we look at Aristotle's teleological metaphysics now, from our modern categorial perspective which embraces 'purpose' in a limited way (Aristotle's 'purpose' does not mean quite what ours does), we see that it has limited workability, that is, we can now say something about its ground, about its fit with reality: it does not fit, or rather, it fits rather badly. We can also see, if we have any sociological and historical sense (which few modern philosophers have), that Aristotle's framework is derived on the model of certain features of the social formation in which he was situated.[11]

The necessity of a categorial structure and its correspondence with reality cannot be shown at the time when it is the reigning categorial structure. Far from being a metaphysical problem which requires philosophical resolution, this is a requirement of any workable categorial structure. The very fact that the methodology functions as the absolute ground of thought on the basis of which problems are defined and answers articulated presents the impossibility, within the terms of that methodology (there are no other terms), of questioning or testing or grounding that methodology itself. But what follows from that? That we **must** find some philosophical way of grounding it which eliminates simple circularity and infinite regress? That is what Hegel supposed (and I think Winfield is right), hence his self-grounding solution which is successful at the expense of eliminating all possibility of open-ended experiential content. The best Hegel can do on this basis is fall back on what has already taken place or what has been revealed by the special sciences as the manifestation of the categorial structure.

The 'systematic' side of Hegel is, then, precisely the side of Hegel which modern science must reject, for the impossibility of grounding the current categorial structure or methodology and the possibility of the admission of new experiential content are two sides of the same coin. Science cannot close itself to new content, therefore it must be impossible to ground the currently reigning methodology. It has been said that this impossibility is a philosophically perplexing one because we are now left with the thing-in-itself. But the thing-in-itself is only a metaphysical designation for a programmatic feature of science, namely the constant possibility of new content. One might say that it is Hegel's preoccupation with eliminating the thing-in-itself that results in the profoundly anti-scientific character of his philosophy.[12]

I think then that we can envisage categorial structures in such a way as to avoid both the epistemological presupposition problem as a **problem** and circular arguments including the Hegelian special kind of circular argument. To summarize: categorial structures are general forms in consciousness of epochal sets of social practices (social formations) but for any specific categorial structure this social groundedness can only be seen from the perspective of the categorial structure which supersedes it.

Thus an epochal critique does not appeal to the (presupposed) 'given facts' which supposedly fall outside any categorial structure but to the inadequacy of the self-grounding of the categories underlying the theory etc. in question and which is now being criticized from a superior categorial vantage-point. As an example of this approach in economics I may mention Marx's. It is often thought, unfortunately by many 'Marxists' as well as non-Marxists and anti-Marxists, that Marx hoped to refute classical economic theory by appealing to the **facts** of capitalist society. Any serious reading of Marx shows this to be a gross misunderstanding. Marx's method does not rest on the presupposition that one can study 'the economic base' as a **datum** independently of any theoretical concepts or categories. When, for example, he criticizes the reigning liberal notion of property he does not do so on the basis of having first independently 'discovered' what property 'really is'. Rather he demonstrates from a new categorial and theoretical vantage-point (in which the category of 'reality' itself has shifted) the inconsistency and incoherence in the classical **concept:** the classical economists admit economically the necessity of the expropriation of the means of production of the labouring majority, an admission which entails a **class** definition of property as capital, while at the same time juridically presenting a universal or **social** (trans-class) definition of property which contradicts the class definition. Again, to take a question which has been misunderstood *ad nauseam,* the immiseration of the labourer is not measured by an absolute standard independently of any specific form of society but only in relation to the capacity and expectations generated in a specific social formation. Says Marx,

> Our wants and pleasures spring from society; we measure them, therefore, by society and not by the objects which serve for their satisfaction. Because they are of a social nature, they are of a relative nature.[13]

We shall see later that the same kind of considerations apply to 'justice'. In each case Marx's object is not **simply** the economic or social **data,** but the theorized data, the limitations of which are thrown into relief for him by adopting the rich categorial structure offered by Hegel's *Logic.*

II Indication/Manifestation or Derivation/Ordering?

The Hegelian systematist (HS) and the Hegelian methodologist (HM) have contrasting conceptions of the manner in which categories, theoretical concepts and empirical data are interrelated. The HM (one who has extracted the categorial structure in the manner I have suggested) moves between these three levels in a manner quite different from that of the HS, even though it is already accepted that both move backwards and forwards between the three levels in some fashion which excludes starting points of the orthodox empiricist (foundations) and rationalist (first principles) varieties.

The difference in the reflective equilibrium (to adapt a term from John Rawls) of philosophical category, theoretical concept and empirical datum of the HM and the HS rests on their different conceptions of the ontological status of the categorial structure. For the HS the categorial structure taken as a pre-ontological realm is at once, as a result of the self-referential character of the second strategic transition, the structure of the natural and social reality and it is absolute. This means that it stands without ontological qualification by (1) observer location in history, and (2) theoretical concepts and empirical data. For the HM, however, the categorial structure can only be said to have a relation to the structure of social and natural reality in so far as it orders theoretical concepts so as to yield workable reflective equilibria and is always open to modification by the two factors mentioned immediately above. The fact that the HM does not actually qualify the categorial structure for long periods, even epochs, is beside the point. That there is a preparedness to do so is an indication of an entirely different and more fruitful conception of the reflective equilibrium.

For the HS theoretical concepts and empirical data (events, entities, actions, processes) are the **manifestation** of that categorial structure and the 'scientist' (Hegelian philosopher) only reveals this structure **in** the data. The scientist, then, is **describing** what is and indeed what must be, given the absolute categorial structure. If the data are themselves manifestations of what is absolute then they too have an absolute character and our theoretical concepts have an absolute character. This must be so even granted that for Hegel all things are relative in the sense that they are not fully realized except in relation to some concrete universal which appears as their end. The data are not able to challenge, through the mediation of challenges to existing theory, the categorial structure in so far as dislocations appear in a specific reflective equilibrium. They merely serve as initial means of access to knowledge of that structure: 'since philosophy is the exploration of the rational, it is for that very reason the apprehension of the present and the actual, not the erection of a beyond...', says Hegel.[14]

For the HM, as conceived here, empirical data may be regarded as a phenomenal (but not thereby unreal) manifestation of essential and veiled entities and processes postulated by theories, but it is not to be supposed that a consequence of this is that they are indirectly a manifestation of the categorial structure. Scientific theories are open and more or less directly structure the contents of the universe in a workable and explanatory way which satisfies the coherence of a specific reflective equilibrium. But the categorial structure is of rather a different nature. It does not directly structure and explain the substance or content of the universe, but is a provisional higher-level system of principles for ordering theoretical concepts. The scientist reveals the content of the universe by **explaining** the data through theoretical concepts which do have ontological import and **ordering** concepts through categories which do not have such import. For example, 'electron', 'gene' and 'surplus-value' are theoretical principles of explanation, while 'universal', 'cause' and 'quality' are categorial principles of order (or form). The two levels should not be conflated - but the HS does precisely that. Certainly, categories may be regarded as only higher level or more general concepts than theoretical concepts. But their distinctiveness as **ordering** rather than **explanatory** concepts is implied by their historically relative **absoluteness,** that is, concepts which form the ground or limit of knowledge cannot be explanatory concepts.

For the HM the philosopher is not, as with the HS, in the act of exploring the rational, apprehending the present and actual but is only (in exploring the rational) exploring **how** the present and actual are presently apprehended - which is quite a different matter. A different task is undertaken by the scientist who is explaining (i.e. directly revealing the structure and inner relation of things) and not simply describing and classifying the particulars of nature and society the substance of which has already been 'proved' to be a universal spirit which unfolds itself through those particulars.

What the substance of things is, is for the scientist not the philosopher to find out. Now, theoretical concepts and categories are regarded as relative, and open to challenge and change. The categorial structures postulated by preliterate societies (personalistic, animistic), by advanced Greek society (Aristotelian, teleological-hierarchical), by seventeenth- and eighteenth-century European society (Cartesian-Newtonian, mechanistic), by nineteenth-century European society (positivistic, evolutionistic) have all been superseded. The crisis of modern Western society is, on the philosophical level, the demand for a new categorial framework, a new system of principles of order, a new reflective equilibrium. It is here that Hegel is still alive.

To narrow down our focus, I think it can be shown, in the light of the foregoing, that Winfield in his prize-winning essay 'Hegel's Challenge to the Modern Economy' is mistaken in thinking that Hegel's **system** as elaborated with special application in the *Philosophy of Right* can provide us with an economic science and policy. Let us take the following question as our point of departure. How are we to understand the relation between justice and the activity human beings enter into as exchangers of commodities? Hegel's system, as expressed in the *Philosophy of Right,* provides an answer to this question and Winfield defends that answer drawing from it prescriptions for the modern economy of the Western world.

Winfield wants to show what kind of economic conditions are necessary for justice to prevail in any society, but wishes to do so in a presuppositionless way. He adopts what he takes to be Hegel's view that relations of commodity exchange are the embodiment of the principle of individual autonomy and freedom on a particularistic level of society. Says Winfield:

> ... what provides the minimal institution of freedom in which interests are reciprocally realized are none other than commodity relations. Hegel comes to this insight by thinking through the basic mandate of civil society, not as naturally construed by liberal theory and political economy, nor as conditioned by some historical necessity, but in accord with the foundation-free requirements of justice.[15]

This principle is a necessary, but not sufficient, condition of justice (or right). Commodity exchange relations fulfil a condition for justice in the social world as we experience it. There can be no justice unless the individual acts with complete freedom of choice, which means in such a way that the action is not determined by any consideration external to the volition, and to so act s/he must act in conditions of mutual respect with other individuals. Such respect can only arise where there is private property. Hegel's description of exchange relations within the realm of 'civil society' is meant to show us both how individual self-determination is a condition of justice and where in the experienced world the embodiment of this condition is manifested. Here is an important qualification: civil society left to itself would generate injustice over a period of time. Commodity exchange relations would allow the development of various inequalities which would undermine the principle of self-determination. Therefore the state intervenes in appropriate ways to maintain exchange relations in their pristine condition, so ensuring justice.

Why should relations of commodity exchange be regarded as the embodiment of a particularistic principle of individual self-determination? Because no exchanger is compelled to hand over his/her property to another; s/he does so completely voluntarily. Moreover, in the act of exchange s/he is the judge of the value of his/her property measured against a possible purchase. Prices are precisely the outcome of all such individual judgements. Also, every exchanger respects every other exchanger as an exchanger, a property-owner like him/herself. Without this mutual respect exchange could not take place at all. Only societies which have attained, through the full exercise of a free market, an adequate level of individual property, respect for property, and individual freedom of choice are societies in which justice is a possibility. Western societies are presently undergoing an encroachment upon property, freedom and mutual respect and therefore justice is under threat. Hegel's system, then, provides a 'challenge to the modern economy'. Winfield warns: 'if the economy does not accord with the concept of just economic relations, what should be altered is not theory, but economic reality'.[16]

What interests me here is the form of the argument. It is assumed that we can know what justice is in its **essentials** before researching the actually existing structures of society in a particular historical period and developing theoretical explanations of social characteristics in reflective equilibrium with these research findings. Of course, Hegel does admit that even philosophy 'presupposes and is conditioned by' empirical studies. But he regards this as only a preliminary, a way of gaining some **indications** of the categorial structure:

> The procedure involved in the formation and preliminaries of a science is not the same as the science itself however, for in this latter case it is no longer experience, but rather the necessity of the Notion, which must emerge as the foundation.[17]

The category of 'freedom', a central category of the *Philosophy of Right,* repeats the category of 'freedom' which is described as the character of all thought in the *Logic.*[18] It is not an empirical enquiry or theoretical explanation in economic or political science which tells us that justice is the realm of freedom, that freedom is the substance and essence of the individual will, that any will expresses 'particular' interests and thus lacks 'universality', and that therefore it must be raised up to the universal in various ways. Civil society, and especially commodity exchange relations, are simply 'discovered' to be one of these ways. These actual relations are taken to be a **manifestation** of this universality working its way out through particulars.

Thus in Hegel we have, as Winfield puts it, 'an economics which falls within the theory of justice'.[19] It is what the fulfilment of the Notion (*Begriff*) requires, i.e. the completion of the process of externalization of the categorial structure, that is crucial here: 'Therefore', Hegel concludes, 'there ought to be a civil society to provide the sphere of freedom for the reciprocal realization of independent interests'.[20]

The form of the argument rules out questions about how the category itself is derived. Certainly there is a kind of logical or dialectical derivation; Hegel climbs a conceptual ladder showing the inadequacy of each rung in getting a proper view of things until the top is reached. But I am not speaking of this kind of derivation. The possibility of a derivation from the world as human beings experience it through reconstructing it at various points in history is not entertained. Instead, experience at various levels is assumed to **indicate** the category, to lead us to it and it can do this, it is supposed, because experience **embodies** the category. Thus if Hegel allows a movement from experience to category, through various mediations, it is one of **indication** and not of **derivation.** Correspondingly, the movement from category to experience, through various mediations, is one of **manifestation** (and embodiment) not of **ordering,** not of providing a kind of *Gestalt* for concepts and data.

We should now ask what are the repercussions of this philosophical system for the progress of economic and social science. This is where we need to probe deeper into the relation of justice and commodity exchange relations. Let us try to understand the reflective equilibrium of category-concept-datum in the manner suggested earlier, which in a sense inverts that of the HS. A different understanding of justice and commodity exchange relations will reveal the limitations of the procedure of the HS.

We may consider the concept of 'justice' to be derived from rather than indicated by commodity exchange relations. We may consider the category of 'freedom' (absolute self-determination) to be derived from rather than indicated by a certain family of general concepts which includes that of 'justice'. We may recall that exchange relations come to dominate activity in societies in a specific historical epoch. We may recall that the particular idea of justice appeared with the development of pervasive exchange relations. Hegel also realizes the importance of these last two facts, it seems, but unlike Hegel we will now entertain the hypotheses that 'justice' is no more than the historically specific derivation in thought of the pervasive commodity exchange relations which we daily encounter in the form of society we are already superseding. We would no longer take it to be the **embodiment** of an eternal and essential category. We will entertain the further hypothesis that the category is a further and more rarefied derivation, a derivation of general concepts such as 'justice'. This makes a world of difference to how we proceed to formulate our conception of commodity exchange relations and of their relation to justice. It throws up a series of fruitful questions and lines of enquiry, and the possibility of expanding the content of economic science in reflective equilibrium, ruled out by the procedure of the HS: the most important, of course, being **how** is 'justice' derived from exchange relations? (See final section below.)

Now, instead of taking the manner of production in a society to be an indication of exchange relations as Hegel does in his 'System of Needs',[21] we ask how do exchange relations as they appear to us order our concepts to give a certain, possibly misleading, interpretation of the deeper production process? Instead of taking exchange to be an indication of justice, we ask how does our concept of 'justice' order our concepts to give a certain, possibly misleading, interpretation of exchange. Conversely, instead of showing how 'justice' embodies itself in exchange relations, and thus considering exchange in the light of our concept of 'justice', we now ask from what features of exchange may the form of 'justice' be derived? Instead of asking what embodies exchange relations and thus considering production in the light of exchange, we ask from what may exchange be derived, that is, what are the historical conditions of its existence? There are empirically specific and open-ended answers to these questions; answers which provide a large number of lines of enquiry, as properly posed scientific questions always do. Hegel's procedure has been inverted.

III Economics and Hegel's Categorial Structure

If I have so far tried to make a general case against Hegel's **system** in the field of economic science, I have now to make a case to support my positive claim: that Hegel's methodology (his categorial structure) stripped of its absolutist ontological pretensions can provide a provisional guide to the ordering of the concepts of economic theory. What I take to be especially important in Hegel's methodology is his unique characterization of how the categories are interrelated, keeping in mind that I am now assuming categories to be the most general and mediated derivatives of our historically specific experience and activity, with no ontological assumptions. This methodology was put to work in economics, broadly conceived, by Karl Marx.

What, it may be wondered, could the HM make of 'Being', the first category of Hegel's logic, in an economic context? For Hegel, 'Being is the indeterminate **immediate**', and it is 'pure indeterminateness and emptiness'.[22] 'Being' is an abstract universal. Its universality is such as to overlook all specific differences. Any science in fact embraces concepts which have something of this character and we can regard 'Being' as a term for the general form of all such concepts. In economics concepts such as 'population', 'society', 'exchange', 'production', taken in their general senses, are of this kind. Such concepts may be taken as starting-points in the sense that they may at least serve to define initially the universe of discourse. But a failure to unfold the specific differences and determinations of 'population' etc. leads to bad science, just as for Hegel a failure to move beyond 'Being', remaining awestruck by its 'truth', is a characteristic of the 'earlier systems' of philosophy which are the 'poorest', such as Parmenides's philosophy of Being.[23] The error this leads to in economics, says Marx, is to take some feature of a historically specific social formation as the feature of all societies or 'human society' in general.[24] More than a century after Hegel and Marx, economists have not fully understood this principle, often being quite content to juggle with empty abstractions, the most notorious of which are probably 'supply' and 'demand'. The point made by Hegel in moving from 'Being' to 'Nothing' is precisely what needs to be understood to understand the **emptiness** of such extremely general concepts which apply to all forms of society.

The concepts of Marx's entire economic theory are ordered by (but only ordered by, not derived from) the categories of Hegel's *Logic*.[25] The fact that Marx largely dropped the Hegelian **terminology** in *Capital* should not deceive us into thinking that he also dropped the categorial methodology itself.[26] But if it is the terminology that convinces us then the *Grundrisse*, a preparatory draft for *Capital*, is the best methodological guide to *Capital*. Take, for example, his use of the Hegelian terms 'posit', 'immediate Being', and 'ground' ('Ground' is a sub-category of 'Essence'). He considers the production of commodities as the 'ground' of exchange and circulation, and in the *Grundrisse* Marx says of circulation:

73

Its immediate being is therefore pure semblance. **It is the phenomenon of a process taking place behind it....** Circulation itself returns back into the activity [production of commodities] which posits or produces exchange-values. It returns into it as into its ground.[27]

Thus he follows Hegel's categorial transition. In explaining the 'Law of Ground', Hegel says:

What **is,** is not to be regarded as a merely **affirmative immediate,** but as something **posited;** we must not stop at immediate determinate being or determinateness as such, but must go back from this into its ground, in which reflection it is a sublated being and is in and for itself.[28]

It is the **character** of the distinction between production and exchange which is defined by Hegelian categories which is possibly Marx's greatest advance over the classical economists such as Smith and Ricardo. The classical economists failed to properly relate them and tended to see the whole economy in terms of the phenomenal exchange level. But it is not surprising that Hegel, the strictly philosophical economist, concerned only with showing how the findings of the economists (and other scientific specialists) could be regarded as manifestations of the internal determinations of Spirit, simply takes over the exchange-dominated political economy of his time. For Hegel cannot allow the economic subject-matter to work out, ultimately, in **its** own way because for him the form of the subject-matter is presupposed in the *Logic.* The economic subject-matter is entirely passive, despite the impression he tries to give at certain points. All the HS can do is show the **agreement** of the findings of economics with the structure already 'proved' in the *Logic.*

It follows that Winfield's revival of Hegelian political economy can only be a revival of the elements of (pre-Marxian) classical political economy selected by Hegel as significant in showing off his *Logic.* Thus Winfield too repeats all the errors of an outdated exchange-dominated economic theory, as we shall see in the next section. Knowledge, for Winfield as for Hegel, does not constantly wait upon the findings of the special sciences; instead the special sciences merely manifest the true knowledge revealed by philosophy. It is because he simply accepts this exchange view of the economy that Hegel sees the economy as the sphere of the Understanding (*Verstand*) in which universality makes a mere 'show'.[29] He does not substantially challenge but simply accepts political economy's point of departure in the view of society as 'System of Needs' or 'economic man'.[30]

To return to the way in which the *Logic* can be made to work, let us take Hegel's category of 'Essence', which is the central category of its main triadic division (that is, Being-Essence-Notion). Essence itself splits into a number of other categories, the broadest of which are 'Essence as Reflection within Itself', 'Appearance' and 'Actuality'. The inversion of Hegel's philosophy means that the category of 'Essence' now operates in quite a different way. To begin with, essence as the 'permanent in things', as Hegel puts it,[31] is not for the HM an **absolutely** permanent but only that which is the framework or parameter of a set of specific kinds of change, a framework which for all we know is itself subject to a more fundamental kind of change. But the dialectical conception of, for example, the interrelation of 'Essence as Reflection within Itself' and 'Appearance' is retained.

If we consider economic phenomena without piercing their forms of 'immediate being', that is, if we operate in ignorance of the distinction between 'Essence as Reflection within Itself' and 'Appearance' (as a principle of conceptual order) we can only treat them as fixed, distinct and abstract and we cannot move beyond the inadequate mode of thought of the 'Understanding'. As a result our subject-matter is invested with the form of abstract universality: the phenomenal forms of what actually turns out to be a specific form of society (namely, capitalist society) are taken to be the essential features of all societies.

'But by dialectic', says Hegel, 'is meant the indwelling tendency outwards by which the one-sidedness and limitation of the predicates of understanding is seen in its true light, and shown to be the negation of them'.[32] This is what Marx's economic project tries to show. Marx attempts to reveal how the 'equality' of exchange is **posited** by a process of surplus-value appropriation which is essentially inegalitarian, how the 'freedom' of commodity exchangers is posited by the essential compulsion over those who own no means of production to sell their labour-power, how the 'private property' which inheres in commodities is the historical appropriation of the means to produce, how the pursuit of personal 'self-interest' is posited by the accumulation of capital, how profit and wages are posited by the splitting of value into two portions, and so on. The essential process posits an appearance which is its opposite; the laws of this process 'become changed into their direct opposite through their own internal and inexorable dialectic', says Marx.[33]

Marx wittily indicates the location of his own (inverted) transition from 'immediate being' to the realm of 'Essence' at the end of Part II of the first volume of *Capital*:

> Let us therefore, in company with the owner of money and the owner of labour-power, leave this noisy sphere, where everything takes place on the surface and in full view of everyone, and follow them into the hidden abode of production, on whose threshold there hangs the notice 'No admittance except on business'.[34]

Having constructed, within 'Essence', a series of theoretical concepts postulating concealed entities and processes, by which to explain the economic and social phenomena (concepts such as 'value', 'surplus-value', 'exchange-value', 'abstract human labour', 'socially necessary labour-time') Marx can then return to the phenomenal level to show vividly **how** the phenomena are the **appearing** to us of those very entities and processes.

A clear illustration of how the category of 'Appearance' functions suggestively in ordering Marx's theoretical concepts is provided by Part VI of the first volume of *Capital* which deals with wages. Marx writes:

> We may therefore understand the decisive importance of the transformation of the value and price of labour itself. All the notions of justice held by both the worker and the capitalist, all the mystifications of the capitalist mode of production, all capitalism's illusions about freedom, all the apologetic tricks of vulgar economists, have as their basis the form of appearance discussed above, which makes the actual relations invisible, and indeed presents to the eye the precise opposite of that relation.[35]

By the category of 'Appearance', with regard to economic theory, I understand not that the essential economic processes are completely hidden (despite Marx's hyperbole above), but that they **manifest** or express themselves, they appear in a form different from their substance. What is 'real' then is not simply what is immediately given to experience (and this is the error of a great deal of modern economics) for this given is **posited**. While for Hegel this positing occurs in the fulfilment of a rational process which **is** the general structure of history and the universe, for Marx (the HM in economics) it is the phenomenal expression of a historical product, a mode of production, which could have been otherwise.[36]

IV Winfield's Errors

Of course I have not satisfactorily argued my positive claim simply by showing that Marx ordered his theoretical concepts with Hegelian categories. At best it might show that such an ordering is possible. It does not show that it results in a superior economic science. The best I can do here is give some hints of this resultant superiority by dealing with some specific misunderstandings of Marx contained in Winfield's essay. His criticisms of Marx are worth taking up, not because they possess any originality, but because they are so widespread. I shall try to show that the misdirection in Winfield's criticisms lies, on the philosophical level, in a failure to appreciate Marx's application of Hegelian methodology. Winfield only attacks Marx for not being a HS and thus completely misses Marx the HM.[37]

Given his interest in defending commodity exchange relations as a necessary condition of freedom and justice, Winfield, drawing on Hegel, rejects Marx's explanation of how commodity exchange relations when dominant (as in capitalist society) entail the treatment of human relations and powers as mere things, that is, commodity fetishism. Winfield's main point is that commodity fetishism does not occur because commodities are not just things but have a social character and this is so because commodities are objects of ownership. 'Consequently', he says, exchangers 'interact not as subjects of things that rule their lives, but as masters of commodities'.[38]

Winfield is proceeding as though Marx says, 'commodities are just things, so don't let them rule your lives'. But Marx is instead claiming that commodities are in essence human relations and powers which **appear** as independent 'things' and that is **how** human beings (both capitalist and worker, in different ways) alienate control over their social life. In particular the treatment of labour-power **as** a thing, at a certain historical point (at which slavery and vassalage are no longer possible), becomes a necessary condition of the automatic and natural appropriation of surplus-value (capitalist exploitation).

While, in this way, exchange relations determine production relations, at the same time the pervasive sphere of exchange of things peculiar to capitalism may be **derived** from the conditions of production which arise at a specific historical juncture, most fundamentally the dispossession from the labouring population of the means of sustaining its own livelihood. Specific relations and forces of production are the 'matter' and relations of exchange are the 'form'. Matter determines a specific form (or range of forms), but the form 'reacts' constituting and sustaining the matter. As Hegel would have it, 'matter' is the 'real **basis** or substrate of form', but 'the **activity of form** through which matter is determined consists in a negative bearing of form towards itself'.[39] Marx says, 'the commodity is both the constant elementary premiss (precondition) of capital and also the immediate result of the capitalist process of production'.[40] Without Hegelian categories, such as 'matter' and 'form', we cannot understand what Marx means by 'commodity fetishism'.

Capitalism, then, is precisely that system in which people are mastered by transforming their productive capacity into commodities, changing it into the form of manipulable things. Thus Marx does not deny that commodities have a social character, rather he asserts it. Capitalist ownership does not prove that human beings as owners master things, but rather the very existence of commodities proves that their own creative capacity has been turned into an object of ownership and hire, sale and purchase on the same level as coats, corn and computers.

A failure to grasp Marx's Hegelian dialectic of whole and part within the category of 'organic unity' is evident in Winfield's extended complaint that on Marx's labour theory of value it is impossible to explain how non-produced goods can and do have value. The labour theory of value is the 'fatal flaw' in Marx's work.[41] He says:

As Hegel has shown, because exchange occurs solely through the free agreement of the owners of the traded commodities, their equivalent exchange value is actually determined by the common resolve of these individuals to exchange them. As a consequence, the exchanged commodities need not be produced nor can the production process of traded commodities have any binding effect on the proportions at which they are bought and sold.[42]

Winfield mentions land and labour-power as examples of such non-produced goods with value.[43] He is unaware, it seems, that Marx's account of how natural forces can have exchange-value is presented in his theory of rent. Now it is true that a piece of land may have had no labour expended on it and therefore **taken in isolation** can have no value in Marx's theory, labour being the substance of value, and the average socially necessary labour-time being the measure of its magnitude. But if the capitalist mode of production dominates agriculture so that land enters into a capitalist market of exchange-values, these being established as signs of the relative magnitudes of labour-time, there is no reason why it should not have an exchange-value and thus be treated **as though** it has value, as having an 'acquired value', if I may call it that. It could only have an exchange-value, and thus be treated as a value, where the law of value prevails.

What interests me here is not so much the economic theory[44] as the methodology. An analogy may help. A plate of iron expands only if it is exposed to heat. Here is a plate which has expanded. But, Winfield would say, this part of the plate has not been exposed to heat but it has expanded, therefore it is not true that a plate of iron expands only if it is exposed to heat. Value, I am suggesting, is a kind of economic 'conductor'. So we need to be careful about what we mean by 'part'. A part of an 'organic whole' cannot be treated as a self-contained entity, the whole then being the sum aggregate of such entities. Says Hegel,

> The external and mechanical relation of whole and parts is not sufficient for us, if we want to study organic life in its truth. And if this be so in organic life, it is the case to a much greater extent when we apply this relation to the mind and the formations of the spiritual world.[45]

Marx speaks of the relation of exchange, distribution, circulation and production as an 'organic whole' and as 'distinctions within a unity'.[46] Commodities as units of exchange are 'parts' of an organic whole, social capital in one of its forms, and are not simply atoms.

When Winfield says that the exchange-value of commodities 'is actually determined by the common resolve of these individuals to exchange them',[47] who can deny that in the economic market people exchange goods because they want to, and they do **agree** to a certain rate of exchange? But this is a merely subjective and formal observation. It may be contrasted, it is true, with situations such as plunder, slavery or corvée in which agreement or contract do not have a role. But it is scientifically important to ask **why** the products of labour and even labour-power itself **must** take the form of commodities for exchange. In other words, it is true that I **want** to exchange this good or that good on this or that occasion for this or that price, but that I enter regularly into some commodity exchange is a matter of absolute necessity and not choice in the present form of society.

Thus the Hegelian dialectic of subjective will and substantial necessity can be seen to enter into the relations of commodity exchange in a way which Winfield, with his one-sided insistence on the subjective freedom of exchangers, does not recognize. Exchange is certainly the interplay of free self-determining agents, but at the same time it rests on the law of value, and this is its substance and its inner necessity.

Then there is Winfield's final statement in the passage above, 'nor can the production process of traded products have any binding effect on the proportions at which they are bought and sold'. It is quite true that the prices of commodities can fluctuate wildly with all kinds of contingencies, such as the 'business sense' of individual traders, the influence of fashion and advertising, and the introduction of competing commodities. But this in no way conflicts with the labour theory of value.[48] Value as a definite magnitude of socially necessary labour-time has a fundamental and **regulative** influence on exchange-values and prices. Marx puts it this way:

> In the midst of the accidental and ever-fluctuating exchange-relations between the products, the labour-time socially necessary to produce them asserts itself as a regulative law of nature. In the same way, the law of gravity asserts itself when a person's house collapses on top of him. The determination of the magnitude of value by labour-time is therefore a secret hidden under the apparent movements in the relative values of commodities. Its discovery destroys the semblance of the merely accidental determination of the magnitude of the value of the products of labour, but by no means abolishes that determination's material form.[49]

Thus the law of value is not immediately evident on the 'surface', in the transactions and fluctuations of the market, but these are nevertheless **generally** determined in form, content and scope as the 'accidents' of the law which is their 'substance', to use Hegel's categories.[50] The law only directly manifests itself in a period of widespread economic crisis.[51]

The failure both to understand the dialectical interrelation of whole and part as organic unity and the regulative nature of the law of value reappears in Winfield's attaching great significance to the fact that 'profit can be made through speculation without any engagement in production'.[52] This, supposedly, proves the falsity of Marx's theory: 'Marx, however, bases his whole theory of the exploitation of labour on the idea that profit cannot arise out of exchange alone'. But of course Marx's theory does allow a profit to arise out of a particular exchange alone. But it can only do so if in **general** surplus-value is being created (i.e. exploitation is taking place). Surplus-value has to be **created** before it can be realized in exchange. Marx is fully aware that prices are not necessarily proportional to the values of commodities, and it is this possibility of a disproportion which makes possible the expansion of value through mere trade. A commodity may, for example, be purchased below its true value and sold above its true value depending on local conditions ('accidents').

V Justice

Hegel's 'justice' is in reality an attempted synthesis of free exchange and state intervention, of individualism and community, and as such it is not a resolution of the contradiction of 'Civil Society' and 'State' but merely a balancing of what **already** is, namely feudal **organic** ties and bourgeois commercial, external and instrumental ones. When Hegel admits that 'civil society affords a spectacle of extravagance and want as well as of the physical and ethical degeneration common to them both'[53] he proposes **amelioration.** For Hegel poverty remains an intractable problem; while Marx suggests it is eradicable but only on condition that exchange itself (and thus so-called 'civil society') **ceases** to be the phenomenal form of the essential appropriation of the labour of others.

Winfield does not get to grips with this question. He insists that justice must be 'foundation-free' or 'self-grounded', which means 'determined by free willing rather than by any independent factors such as natural law or the given nature of the self' or by 'a structure they have not willed into being'. And, 'since freedom is the substance of justice, the philosophy of right has as its subject matter nothing but the self-determined reality of the freedom of individuals, which Hegel appropriately calls the Idea of the free will, in so far as the Idea is self-determination *per se*'. [54]

Winfield's argument, then, runs along the by now familiar line that any attempt to ground justice (conventionalism, natural rights theory, etc.) throws up the presupposition problem, this time with an ethical or political (in the broad sense) content. This may be avoided in so far as we accept Hegel's special circular argument in which justice is the manifestation in the phenomenal realm of Objective Spirit of the Idea of freedom which has already been 'proved' in a presupposition-less way in the *Logic*. It seems that for Winfield only a self-grounded concept of justice can provide a genuine critique of modern society. When he goes so far as to say that if 'modern relations ... do not accord with concepts of right, a revolution may be called for

80

not in the science of justice, but in existing institutions'[55] this seems quite un-Hegelian to me, or at least un-Winfieldian in so far as it seems to presuppose the very transcendental concepts which Winfield's foundation-free justice was supposed to avoid.

Still, the question of his interpretation of Hegel is not my principal concern, as I have said. Instead, I shall suggest that far from providing the only possible genuine critique of modern society, the self-grounding approach of the HS can provide no critique at all (as I think Hegel himself recognized, with a few lapses). The only possible critique is a grounded one, one which emerges by seeing the ground of the previously ungroundable in thought, in this case the ground of liberalism in exchange-relations as the phenomenal form of capitalist production relations. This ground exhibits itself in the shift from the atomistic and causalist categorial structure of the political economists (Mill, Smith, Ricardo, *et al.*) to the Hegelian dialectical one espoused by Marx.

Marx's outline account of justice takes account of the presupposition problems in the way I explained earlier.[56] One may say that the ethical critique of capitalism is, for Marx, capitalism's ethical self-critique. It is not a critique from some **externally** presupposed moral standpoint, but one presented by the terms of capitalism themselves. Marx could see this in so far as his standpoint was that of a capitalism already beginning to supersede itself. It is worth quoting at length a passage from the third volume of *Capital* which is not as well known as it deserves to be:

> The justice of transactions between agents of production consists in the fact that these transactions arise from the relations of production as their natural consequence. The legal forms in which these economic transactions appear as voluntary actions of the participants, as the expression of their common will and as contracts that can be enforced on the parties concerned by the power of the state, are mere forms that cannot themselves determine their content. They simply express it. The content is just so long as it corresponds to the mode of production and is adequate to it. It is unjust as soon as it contradicts it. Slavery, on the basis of the capitalist mode of production, is unjust; so is cheating on the quality of commodities.[57]

Subjectively, production relations are historically given, so that the position I find myself born into (class mobility is not denied, but is insignificant) appears to me, indeed in a sense **is,** natural. Thus the exchange of labour for wages is natural, and it cannot appear as unjust but only as the natural framework **within** which questions of justice may arise. Thus a particular wage may be deemed unjust, but not wages as such; to pass off an adulterated commodity is unjust, but that products should appear in the form of commodities is not considered unjust.

The very content of 'justice' in capitalist society is given by the phenomenal form of commodity exchange which, impressing us immediately in our daily lives, has come to be the 'type' of all social relations. The parameters of this form are: freedom because apparently no coercion is involved, equality because the principle of equivalence in exchange is adhered to, and mutual respect because the exchange requires ownership. But this form tells us nothing about the conditions under which human products can become commodities. We cannot arrive at the essential content from the form alone, although we can derive the form from the historical content. In an economic theory which is an adequate reflective equilibrium of economic data, theoretical concepts and Hegelian categories, this content reveals itself to be essentially inegalitarian (wages are not equivalent to the value created), and coercive (the wage-earner **must** sell and continually re-sell his/her labour-power). As for respect for persons - it turns out to be the 'show' of class oppression.[58]

Commodity exchange relations give rise in thought to freedom, equality, property and respect for persons as the defining features of justice and by these same tokens the relations revealed by the HM's critique of bourgeois economic theory, given some historical 'distance', may be judged to be unjust, i.e. unfree, unequal, exploitative and oppressive. Thus **by its own standards** this social formation is unjust despite its historically typical claim of justice. Capitalism stands self-condemned. Here is the meaning of Marx's insistence on the **intrinsic** hypocrisy of capitalist society.

If we are still tempted by the question, 'What then is **the** concept of justice?', one can only respond with a programme for bringing the **form** of justice presented by capitalism into capitalism's substantive **content.** Thus the non-capitalist society of the future can only be achieved in thought by the standards of capitalism itself. What its own standards will turn out to be awaits the real achievement of such a society.

Notes

I am grateful for comments and criticisms of an earlier version from William L. McBride (Purdue University), David P. Levine (University of Denver), Chris Arthur (University of Sussex) and an anonymous reader for *Explorations in Knowledge.* A special thanks is due to Richard Dien Winfield (University of Georgia) for his generous and helpful response to my request for his comments on the earlier version.

1. A set of categories which, most importantly, indicates where the limitations of causal explanation and quantification lie, limitations which mainstream economics has shown itself at a complete loss in recognizing. I do not deal with this matter here, but try to broach the subject in my 'Two methodological

paradigms in development economics', in *The Philosophical Forum*, vol. 18, no. 1 (1986).

2. His essay entitled 'Hegel's Challenge to the Modern Economy' now appears in Robert L. Perkins (ed.), *History and System: Hegel's Philosophy of History,* State University of New York Press, Albany, 1984. With this essay Winfield was the winner of a prize for the best submission on the theme 'Hegel on Economics and Freedom' in a competition endowed by the Roe Corporation of South Carolina and organized by the Hegel Society of America for its Seventh Biennial Meeting, October 1982.

3. Cf. Colletti, L., *Marxism and Hegel,* NLB, London, 1973.

4. See his 'The Route to Foundation-Free Systematic Philosophy', *The Philosophical Forum,* vol. 15, no. 3 (1984); 'Conceiving Reality without Foundations: Hegel's Neglected Strategy for *Realphilosophie',* *The Owl of Minerva,* vol. 15, no. 2 (1984).

5. Hegel takes pains at several points in his work to explain that if logic is the science of 'thought' this is thought in quite a different sense from the standard one. It is not 'subjective, arbitrary and accidental' or the 'mere forms of thought', but the science of spirit, truth, God, the eternal, the absolute. See *HL,* §19 and *Zusatz.*

6. Dialectical materialism as originated by Engels and Plekhanov is the direct result of **applying** the *Logic* without concern for the presupposition problems. Marx's method is not dialectical materialism.

7. *SLM,* p. 843.

8. Criticizing Hegel's philosophy, Marx says, 'Just as nature lay enclosed in the thinker in a shape which even to him was shrouded and mysterious, as an absolute idea, a thing of thought, so what he allowed to come forth from himself was simply this **abstract nature,** nature as a thing of thought - but with the significance now of being the other-being of thought, real, intuited nature as distinct from abstract thought'. 'Economic & Philosophical Manuscripts', in *Early Writings,* trans. R. Livingstone, Penguin, Harmondsworth, 1975, pp. 398-9..

9. *PM,* p. 86.

10. It works less well in respect of nature for there is no reason to suppose that the categories which reflect social structures should also reflect natural structures. When categorial

structures are **freely** elaborated science too will be free of the limitations of models which are socially conditioned and of the resistance to utterly novel ideas which lack the 'familiarity' of society-based models.

11. I realize this is a very big claim. As big claims require big justifications if they are to convince anyone, I do not propose to attempt a justification in a few sentences. A separate work is required.

12. Cf. *SLM*, pp. 489-90, for example.

13. *Wage Labour and Capital*, Progress, Moscow, 1979, p. 33.

14. *HPR*, Preface, p. 10.

15. Perkins, *History and System*, p. 228.

16. Ibid., p. 221. Winfield's interpretation of Hegel at this point, as at several others, makes me uncomfortable, but in this essay I shall concern myself hardly at all with the question of the adequacy of his interpretation.

17. *Philosophy of Nature*, trans. M.J. Petry, Allen & Unwin, London, 1970, §246 remark.

18. For example, *HL*, §23.

19. Perkins, *History and System*, p. 221.

20. Ibid., p. 227.

21. *HPR*, §§189-208; note esp. §§199-201.

22. *SLM*, pp. 81-82.

23. See *HL*, §86 *Zusatz*.

24. Marx's 1857 'Introduction' is very instructive on this point. It is included in the *Grundrisse*, trans. M. Nicolaus, Penguin, Harmondsworth, 1973.

25. Lenin was not exaggerating when he said, 'it is impossible completely to understand Marx's *Capital* and especially its first chapter, without having thoroughly studied and understood the whole of Hegel's *Logic*. Consequently half a century later none of the Marxists understood Marx!' *Collected Works*, Progress, Moscow, 1970, vol. 38, p. 180.

26. When Marx says in the Postface to the second edition of *Capital,* vol. I, that he 'here and there in the chapter on the theory of value coquetted with the mode of expression peculiar to him [Hegel]' (*Capital,* vol. I, Penguin, Harmondsworth, 1976, p. 103), I take this to imply that the **terminology** of Hegel was largely dropped (except for the coquetting) in *Capital* (but not in *Grundrisse*), not that Hegel's categorial methodology was.

27. *Grundrisse,* p. 255 (Marx's emphasis).

28. *SLM,* p. 446 remark.

29. *HPR,* §189.

30. Cf. Hunt, G., 'Gramsci's Marxism and the concept of *Homo oeconomicus', International Studies in Philosophy,* vol. 17, no. 1 (1985), pp. 11-23.

31. *HL,* §112 remark.

32. *HL,* §81.

33. *Capital,* vol. I, p. 729.

34. Ibid., pp. 279-80.

35. Ibid., p. 680.

36. It should be clear on this basis that Marx is no more a materialist in the ordinary philosophical sense than Hegel, at least on a Hegelian reckoning, is an idealist. It is unfortunate that Martin Nicolaus, the Marxist scholar who produced the first adequate English edition of the *Grundrisse,* a key work in understanding Marx's Hegelian methodology, should write in his Foreword that Hegel 'denied the **reality** of what the senses perceive', op. cit., p. 27.

37. I may admit that in some cases Winfield's errors do not need to be seen as flowing from his HS position but more simply from an ignorance of Marx's economics.

38. Perkins, *History and System,* p. 235.

39. *SLM,* pp. 450, 453.

40. The 'circular nature' of the argument is explained by Marx in the opening pages of the 'Results of the Immediate Process of Production', reproduced as an Appendix in *Capital,* vol. I, p. 948ff. This quotation is from p. 949.

41. Perkins, *History and System,* p. 236.

42. Ibid., p. 235. The same point is made on p. 234 and is supported with a reference to Böhm-Bawerk's famous critique of Marx's theory with no mention of the important refutations of that critique, especially R. Hilferding, 'Böhm-Bawerk's Criticism of Marx', in Sweezy, P. (ed.), *Karl Marx and the Close of His System,* Merlin Press, London, 1975.

43. Perkins, *History and System,* p. 234. It is simply false to claim that labour-power is non-produced. Muscle and brain must be sustained, and the goods which sustain them have value precisely because of the labour embodied in them. It is the difference between the value of labour-power (wages) and the value produced by the labour realized from the labour-power that accounts for surplus-value and the very possibility of profit. The value produced by labour is greater than the value of the labour-power that yields that labour.

44. For a clear summary of Marx's rent theory, see Bernice Shoul, 'Karl Marx's Solutions to Some Theoretical Problems of Classical Economics', in Howard, M.C. and King, J.E., *The Economics of Marx,* Penguin, Harmondsworth, 1976, pp. 154-160.

45. *HL,* §135 remark.

46. *Grundrisse,* pp. 99-100.

47. Perkins, *History and System,* p. 235. Also, 'the exchange-value of any product bears no necessary relation to the amount of labour expended in its production, but rather depends on the wills of its prospective buyers' (pp. 236-7).

48. One may add that the exchange-values of certain commodities may change while their values remain constant or vice versa, as Marx explains, *Capital,* vol. I, p. 146.

49. Ibid., p. 168.

50. See Hegel, *SLM,* pp. 555-57.

51. For a clear, if contested, account of the way in which the law of value expresses itself in crisis, see Mattick, P., *Economic Crisis and Crisis Theory,* Merlin Press, London, 1981.

52. Perkins, *History and System,* p. 236.

53. *HPR,* §185.

54. Winfield, R.D., 'The Theory and Practice of the History of Freedom: On the Right of History in Hegel's Philosophy of Right', also in Perkins, *History and System,* p. 129.

55. Ibid., p. 126.

56. The question of what can be made of justice in the context of Marx's theory has recently given rise to a lively debate. For example, see Cohen, M., Nagel, T. and Scanlon, T., (eds), *Marx, Justice and History,* Princeton University Press, 1980.

57. Marx, *Capital,* vol. III, Penguin, Harmondsworth, 1981, pp. 460-61.

58. Cf. Hunt, G., 'The anatomy of civil society', *Proceedings of the XVII World Congress of Philosophy,* Section 2a, Montreal, 1983; and 'The development of the concept of civil society in Marx', in *History of Political Thought,* forthcoming (1987).

5 The Metamorphosis of Judaism in Hegel's Philosophy of Religion

PETER C. HODGSON

I Introduction

Hegel's treatment of Judaism in his early theological writings and in his lectures on the philosophy of world history is relatively well-known. One of the best and most recent discussions of it is found in Shlomo Avineri's paper, 'The Fossil and the Phoenix: Hegel and Krochmal on the Jewish Volksgeist', presented at the 1982 biennial meeting of the Hegel Society of America.[1] Avineri points out that Hegel's portrayal of Judaism in the early writings mainly followed the conventional image found in traditional Christian theology. He depicted Judaism as a religion of 'slavish obedience to laws' laid down not by the people themselves but by a 'supreme wisdom on high', as well as a religion of deceit, cowardice, alienation, and stubborn particularism.[2] In one significant instance, however, Hegel deviated from these traditional stereotypes, namely in his understanding of and sympathy for the political, national feelings of the Jews during the period of Roman subjugation prior to the destruction of the second temple. They 'discarded their ineffective messianic hopes and took up arms', resisting courageously but suffering 'the most appalling of human calamities', the loss of city and nation. 'The scattered remnant of the Jews have not abandoned the idea of the Jewish state, but they have reverted not to the banners of their own courage, but only to the standards of an ineffective messianic hope'.[3]

This deviation, though isolated, indicates that Hegel's views on Judaism were ambivalent. While sharing for the most part the traditional Christian bias, he was unwilling to accept the view that the destruction of the temple was a divine punishment visited upon the Jews for their rejection of Jesus, and he insistently advocated a liberal policy on the question of granting civil and political rights to contemporary Jews.[4] This policy, together with the observation that 'the Jews have not abandoned the idea of the Jewish state', entailed a recognition of the survival of the Jewish people and the Jewish religion. Yet Hegel was unable to account for this survival philosophically - which points, according to Avineri, to the central ambiguity in his portrayal of Judaism in the *Lectures on the Philosophy of World History*. In these lectures he virtually ignored the political history of Judaism, biblical as well as postbiblical, and made no attempt to explain how and why the Jewish people, unable as they were in his view to develop viable political institutions, could continue to exist as a distinct, identifiable group after their great world-historical mission was accomplished - the contribution of the idea of monotheism to religious consciousness. 'The Jews thus remain, for Hegel, in some way in history but not of history, a fossil - yet a living organism'.[5] Yet Nachman Krochmal, an obscure early nineteenth-century Jewish scholar living in Eastern Galacia, performed an *Aufhebung* of Hegel's views on Judaism from within the framework of an Hegelian philosophy of history: in virtue of the universality and spirituality of the idea of monotheism, the Jewish people, claimed Krochmal, are the true bearers of absolute spirit and thus have been able to transcend the temporality of history, being reborn like the legendary phoenix after every defeat, while all other nations eventually disappeared along with their particular spiritualities.[6]

Despite its ambivalence, the portrayal of Judaism in the philosophy of history lectures was reasonably consistent and coherent. The same cannot be said for the *Lectures on the Philosophy of Religion*, the first of the posthumously edited lectures to be published by Hegel's students and friends shortly after his death; consequently, the philosophy of religion has always proved frustrating to scholars attempting to evaluate Hegel's interpretation of Judaism. The consistency of the philosophy of history lectures is attributable to the fact that the parts dealing with Judaism are very likely based on auditors' notebooks of Hegel's last two courses on this subject, those of 1828-29 and 1830-31.[7] The philosophy of religion, on the other hand, amalgamated materials from Hegel's four lecture series on religion - 1821, 1824, 1827, and 1831 - into an editorially constructed text that totally obscured the significant structural and substantive differences introduced by Hegel each of the times he addressed this topic.

Our new edition of the *Lectures on the Philosophy of Religion* [8] for the first time separates and reconstructs Hegel's four lecture series, presenting them as independent units on the basis of a complete re-editing of the available sources. When the sections on Judaism are studied in sequence, it becomes evident that Hegel's treatment undergoes a striking metamorphosis, mostly in the direction of a more favourable and sympathetic assessment, although the ambivalence of his attitude is by no means completely resolved. Hegel seems to be struggling to overcome inherited cultural prejudice, but he finally remains uncertain about the place of Judaism in the history of religions. In what follows, I shall simply trace the trajectory of Hegel's interpretation in the successive lectures, thus hoping to displace the confusion that is present in the old edition, as well as to show that Hegel's struggle with Judaism continued to the end. Rather than being a fossil, it proved after all to be a phoenix for Hegel, arising in a new shape each time he turned his attention to it. Emil Fackenheim, commenting on Karl Rosenkranz's remark that Judaism was for Hegel a 'dark riddle', which both attracted and repelled him throughout his life, observes that 'Jewish existence, supposedly rendered anachronistic by the Christian world if indeed not by classical antiquity, keeps reappearing in Hegel's thought'.[9] The deep question, which this paper can only very partially attempt to answer, is why this should be the case and what shapes Judaism assumes.

First a word about Hegel's sources. He relied almost entirely on his own reading of the Hebrew scriptures, which in the first three lectures was limited to the 'Books of Moses' (the Pentateuch), Job, and the Psalms. He had long been attracted to Job as 'the philosopher of Mosaic antiquity' through the influence of his teachers in the Tübingen seminary as well as J.G. Herder's *The Spirit of Hebrew Poetry* (1787). In 1831 he alluded specifically to the universalism of the 'later prophets', that is, Second and Third Isaiah and Haggai, as well as to certain passages in the Psalms, although references to the implicit universalism of Israelite faith were already found in 1824. While Hegel made use of a few recently published biblical commentaries, it is clear that he was unfamiliar with any of the Jewish extrabiblical writings - the Mishna, the Talmud, the Midrashic literature - and did not attend in any way to the postbiblical history of Judaism; this, as Avineri points out, is one of the chief defects of his treatment.

II Hegel's Lecture Manuscript of 1821

In all but the last lectures, Judaism ('the religion of sublimity') is discussed along with Greek religion ('the religion of beauty') in the second main division of *Determinate Religion*. There are, however, some important variations in the order of their treatment, which I shall describe in due course. The 'great thesis' of Jewish religion, says Hegel at the outset, is that God is one God: the personal One (*der Eine*), not the neuter One (*das Eine*), not substance but subject, the infinite reflected into itself as singular and concrete universality. This God is all-powerful, and the sublimity of his power is such that it is expressed representationally not by physical force but by the pure word, which is pure light: 'God said, Let there be light, and there was light, . . . light that is only a breath' (pp. 128-129, 134-137). By contrast, the contingency and dependence of the world are expressed in the doctrines of creation, preservation and passing away. God's power in relation to the world remains **undetermined**: it does not acquire a determinate content, end, or purpose, other than the exercise of power as such, and the distinction between the goodness and the justice of God is ignored. God is 'not yet inwardly concrete, not yet elaborated within himself', but is merely **abstract power,** the being-for-self of the One (pp. 137-139). The paradigmatic portrayal of the God of abstract power is found, according to Hegel, in the Book of Job. The divine majesty and inscrutability portrayed in Job demand absolute submission on the part of human beings, 'fear of the Lord'. To be sure, God acts to bring soul out from the pit of Sheol, but this act of justice or mercy is also merely an expression of divine power. In the end, it is submission to the Lord that restores Job to his former happiness (pp. 140-141).

The Jewish cultus, in Hegel's view, is a fundamental expression of the servile consciousness and of the master-servant relationship (pp. 152-160). When God is comprehended only under the abstract category of the One, and not as dialectically self-mediated, then 'this human lack of freedom' is the result, and 'humanity's relationship to God takes the form of a heavy yoke, of onerous service. True liberation is to be found in Christianity, in the Trinity'. The condition of servitude is to have one self-consciousness solely in the other and on behalf of the other. 'Fear of the Lord is the absolutely religious duty, to regard myself as nothing, to know myself only as absolutely dependent - the consciousness of the servant vis-à-vis the master'. What God demands is that his people should have 'the basic feeling of their dependence'. Here we encounter the first of Hegel's several allusions in the 1821 manuscript to Schleiermacher's just-published *Glaubenslehre* (pp. 158n, 218n), and it is noteworthy that he regards Schleiermacher's famous description of religious consciousness as the 'feeling of absolute dependence' to be an expression of Jewish (and later of Roman) rather than of Christian piety.

If one has one's self-consciousness only in and through absolute dependence on the Lord, then there is also a sense in which one is absolutely re-established in relationship to the Lord - a relationship that is singular, unique and exclusive. Hegel thinks this is the source of Jewish 'obstinacy' and 'particularity', the conviction that the Jewish people alone are God's people, and that he alone is their God.

This portrayal of Judaism still shares the interpretative perspective of the *Early Theological Writings* and the *Phenomenology of Spirit,* [10] even though new categories and themes have appeared. As Reinhard Leuze suggests, Hegel has placed a different valuation on essentially the same characterization of Judaism.[11] While the master-servant relationship was earlier viewed as a primary instance of human self-alienation, it is now seen as implicit in the concept of God as abstract power. At the same time, a basis is laid for the quite different interpretation of Judaism that will appear in 1824; for already in 1821 Hegel alludes to the fact that the power of the Lord is **wisdom,** and he recognizes that a **reconstitution** of the self in the One occurs through 'fear of the Lord'.

III The Lectures of 1824

In these lectures, the fundamentally negative cast of the treatment just three years earlier is replaced by a more balanced and fully developed assessment. The introduction of the categories of wisdom and purpose, mandated by the general reconception of the religions of spiritual individuality (Jewish, Greek, and Roman) in 1824, has something to do with this reinterpretation, but basically it seems to be the result of a deeper and more appreciative evaluation of the literature of the Hebrew Bible on Hegel's part.

After a brief reference to the metaphysical concept of God in Judaism - the 'infinitely important' recognition that God is simply and solely One, which is the ground of the absolute spirituality of God, 'the path to truth' (pp. 425-426) - Hegel turns to the 'divine self-determination' as depicted representationally in the form of creation and preservation (pp. 426-438). God is not the result of the creative process - this is no theogony, an issuing forth of the gods - but the starting point; and, as distinct from human production, this is an absolute creation, *ex nihilo,* an inner, 'intuitive', eternal activity on God's part. God's creation and preservation of the world show forth his goodness and justice, indicating that what is at work here is **infinite, purposive wisdom,** not just abstract, indeterminate power (as Hegel thought in 1821). Created things are regarded as prosaic, stripped of divinity, devoid of autonomy, and the externality of nature is clearly recognized. This de-divinization of nature is a necessary step toward a valid understanding of the relationship of God and world. In Jewish religion this relationship is understood essentially in terms of God's **sublimity** (*Erhabenheit*). Sublimity means that God is exalted above the reality in which he appears, and that the reality itself is negated or totally subjected to God's power. Thus God creates by means of a word, which immediately passes away.

God's purpose vis-à-vis the world is ethical, no longer natural, and has its seat in human self-consciousness and freedom. But we are still at the stage of immediate, natural ethical life, and hence the family is the ethical form in which the divine purpose is realized - this one family, the Jewish people, to the exclusion of all others. Here we encounter the striking, 'infinitely difficult' contradiction that is present in Jewish religion: on the one hand God is universal, the God of all humanity ('all peoples are called upon to recognize him and glorify his name', Ps. 117:1-2), but on the other hand his purposes and operations are so limited as to be confined to just this one people, defined by birth and race. For this reason, in Hegel's view, the universal content of the story of the creation and fall of humanity in Genesis 1-3 became disconnected from subsequent

Jewish piety. Jewish particularity, however, is not polemical or fanatical (as in Islam), because there is no obligation to convert other peoples to the God of Israel.

The cultus of Jewish religion (pp. 441-452) has both negative and affirmative aspects. The negative aspect is fear, fear of the Lord. But - and this is where 1824 departs decisively from the 1821 manuscript - this is no earthly lord that is feared. It is rather fear of the absolute, in which everything ephemeral and contingent is given up and through which one is elevated to the level of pure thought. Hence fear of the Lord **is the beginning of wisdom.** 'Wisdom' means not taking anything particular to be absolute and substantive; it means recognizing the relativity of all that is finite. Hence **this** fear of the Lord entails a fundamental **liberation** from all earthly forms of bondage, a letting everything go, an immersion in the Lord. 'It is the intuition of pure, absolute power, . . . abstracting absolutely from everything particular. Consequently it is not at all what is termed a "feeling of dependence"'. Whereas in the manuscript Judaism was viewed precisely as an embodiment of Schleiermacher's definition of religious piety, now it is just the reverse: Judaism is the first of the religions of freedom, and Schleiermacher's version of religion as dependence is reserved solely for the Romans (p. 443, esp. n. 551).

The affirmative side of Jewish worship arises directly from what has just been said. The fear of the Lord that is the beginning of wisdom yields an absolute trust, an infinite faith, which passes over into a distinctive kind of existence. This trust 'is preserved through so many great victories, which are emphasized also in Christianity. It is this trust, this faith of Abraham's, that causes the history of this people to carry on' (p. 446). Such an assessment represents a dramatic shift from the portrayal of Abraham and his people in *The Early Theological Writings,* and Hegel has hit upon a clue to the question of the survival of Judaism. But he does not pursue the clue; he leaves it with this one sentence. As I have pointed out, Hegel nowhere takes into account the history of this people; his treatment is limited to what he regards as the oldest biblical expressions of Israelite faith. Judaism is not viewed as a living religion; for that matter, no other religions are either, except for Christianity.

IV The Lectures of 1827

The interpretative trajectory of 1824 reaches its zenith in the lectures of 1827. This is signalled immediately by the reversal of order in which the two religions comprising the second section of *Determinate Religion* are treated, so that now Greek religion is considered first and Jewish religion second. In 1827 the problematic of this section is defined as 'the elevation of the spiritual above the natural', but the elevation occurs in different ways in the two religions. For Greek religion, the natural element is taken up and transfigured in free subjectivity, but it is not purified of its externality and sensibility, so that this religion is still tinged by

93

finitude: the gods are represented by the sensibly beautiful human shape, and they are many. For Jewish religion the sensible element is left behind; it is ruled and negated by the one God who is infinite subjectivity and subsists without shape, only for thought, the God who is sublimely free spirit in relation to the natural world. Judaism, then, is the more purely spiritual religion. In this distinction, concludes Hegel at the beginning of the section on Jewish religion, lies 'the necessity of the elevation of the religion of beauty into the religion of sublimity', namely, 'that the particular spiritual powers, the ethical powers, should be embraced in a spiritual unity' (pp. 640-642, 559).

In the two earlier lectures, the relationship between Jewish and Greek religion was considered as mutually complementary rather than as progressive; Hegel never referred to the 'elevation' of one into the other. This is evident from the organization of the manuscript, in which the representational and cultic forms of the two religions are subordinated to an inclusive scheme, even though the portrayal of Jewish religion is considerably less attractive there than the portrayal of Greek. Likewise, the dialectical structure of the 1824 lectures resists a linear or progressive development among the determinate religions (see the Editorial Introduction, pp. 45-46).

That Hegel should now speak of the 'elevation' of the religion of beauty into the religion of sublimity seems to follow in part from his continuing and increasingly favourable reassessment of Judaism, but it may also be related to the polemical context of the 1827 lectures, namely Hegel's defence against the charge of pantheism and atheism brought against him by the Neopietists.[12] Here he clearly aligns himself with Jewish monotheism. Monotheism is in fact close to the authentic insight of Oriental and Spinozistic pantheism, in Hegel's view. When evaluating the Buddhist concept of nirvana in 1827, Hegel argues that there is an essential truth in the Oriental intuition of the universal - not the spurious claim that 'all is God [*alles Gott sei*]', which would be an apotheosis of finite things, but rather the truth that 'the All is God', 'the All that remains utterly one [*das All, das schlechthin eins bleibt*]' and thus is the **negativity** of finite things. The 'pan' of pantheism is to be taken as universality (*Allgemeinheit*), not as totality (*Allheit*). This is the essential truth that was grasped by Spinoza, despite the 'babblers' who accuse him of atheism (pp. 572-575). The several appreciative references to (the Jewish philosopher) Spinoza in the 1827 lectures, in the context of the pantheism-atheism debate, may have helped to lead Hegel to a more appreciative evaluation of Judaism as well.

But the 'advance' from Greek to Jewish religion is not undialectical, even in 1827. Judaism may not be tinged with finitude, but neither is finitude transfigured and overreached by infinitude in it. Moreover, the one universal God of Judaism is believed to be the God of a particular people. At the beginning of the section on Roman religion, Hegel refers to the 'one-sidedness' of both Greek and Jewish religion, and this in fact seems closer to his actual view (p. 688). It is only from particular perspectives that one appears as 'higher' than the other. From the point of view of the idea of God, monotheism, and spiritual unity and subjectivity, Judaism is higher. But from the point of view of the mediation of divinity and humanity (i.e., incarnation), as well as of free ethical institutions, Greek religion is higher. Their respective one-sidednesses are finally overcome, not in Roman religion, which proves to be an abortive and retrograde, arbitrary and expedient, unification of the religions, but in the Christian religion. (Yet, are not Christian claims to finality equally 'perspectival'?)

Nearly the whole of the 1827 discussion of Judaism is devoted to a careful analysis of the Jewish idea of God and to various aspects of the relationship of God and world (pp. 670-683). This material is already present in 1824, but it is reworked, expanded, and presented more clearly. The great contribution of Israel to the history of religion is its comprehension of the 'spiritually subjective unity' of God. This subjective unity is not mere substance but is absolute power, wisdom, and purpose, for which reason it is 'holy', it merits the name 'God' for the first time. It is in fact 'infinite subjectivity', which is the highest philosophical concept; as such, God subsists without sensible shape, only for thought.

But this one God does not remain in self-enclosed, abstract identity with himself. Rather God's wisdom contains the process of 'divine particularization' (a description reserved to Greek religion in 1824), that is, divine self-determining, judging, creating. This process is not yet posited **within** God concretely but remains abstract and external; it is not yet an immanent Trinity. But the act of creation is a highly important, in fact definitive, determination of the Jewish God, having several implications for both the world and God. First, the world does not emanate from God, as in Hindu and Greek cosmogonies, but is created *ex nihilo*. This means that the subjectivity of the One remains what is absolutely first and is not superseded by what has gone forth. Second, God's relations to the world - the more specific moments of divine wisdom, which are goodness and justice - are definitive of God's own being, so that (contra Schleiermacher) we do in fact **know God** in knowing his relations. The categories of goodness and justice are now defined more fully. As good, God releases and sets free from himself the created world; only what is genuinely free can do this, can let its determinations go as free, can release them to 'go their separate ways', which is the totality of the finite world. As just, God maintains the world in relation to himself, does not abandon it to radical autonomy, specifies its purpose. Third, the world is rendered profane, prosaic; nature is divested of divinity, and there is no spurious identity of finite and infinite. The manifestation of God in the world takes on the character of sublimity, which is its genuine form, or of miracle, which is specious. Finally, God's purpose is made manifest in the natural and human worlds. This purpose is simply that the whole earth and all peoples should proclaim the glory of God. Such glorification of God is the 'inner aspect' of all human activity, and it is what underlines the 'remarkable' faith of the Jewish people.

At the end of this perceptive analysis of the Jewish idea of God, Hegel briefly mentions certain 'limitations' (pp. 683-686). These are principally three: the self-determining wisdom of God is not yet an inward self-development (the idea of God as 'what is eternally self-developing within itself' is found only in the revelatory religion); despite the implicit universalism, the God of Judaism remains a national God, the God of a limited national family rather than of the whole human family; and the divine purposes are abstract because they are simply commandments given by God as something prescribed and immutable, rather than purposes worked out in the conflict and dialectic of historical/ethical life. While this does present the substance of Hegel's case against Judaism, the criticisms are muted and non-polemical; and the portrayal as a whole is fair and balanced.

V The Lectures of 1831

For the last lectures, Hegel undertook a radical structural revision of *Determinate Religion.* All of the Near Eastern religions are now grouped together as transitional forms at the beginning of the third and final section, 'the religion of freedom' (or 'reconciliation'), which does not reach its consummation in any of the determinate religions but only in Christianity. The Near Eastern religions include the religions of the good (Persian and Jewish), the religion of anguish ('Phoenician'), and the religion of ferment (Egyptian). The religion of anguish, which makes its appearance for the first time in 1831, is a construct derived by Hegel from classical mythology, relating to the figure of Adonis and focusing on the symbol of the phoenix bird, which immolates itself, then rises reborn from the ashes; it is not Phoenician religion in any historical sense, although Hegel seems to have thought that it was (see pp. 452n-455n). Thus it was Hegel himself who introduced the figure of the phoenix, but it was Krochmal who showed that it properly applies to Judaism, not to an imaginary religion that supposedly represents a dialectical advance beyond Judaism.

Judaism is introduced into the discussion through the category of the good, which, as we have seen, already assumed in 1827 greater significance as a divine predicate. In Judaism, by contrast with Persian religion, the good is 'for itself' in such a way as to belong to the essence of the substance of God, to constitute the substance as free, personal, and subjective for the first time (pp. 738-739). The analysis then proceeds along the lines of the 1827 lectures. Only toward the end do we arrive at the innovative feature of the 1831 presentation. The antithesis of good and evil is grounded for Judaism neither in a cosmic dualism (the theogonic myth, exemplified for Hegel by Persian religion) nor in absolute substance (the tragic myth, as represented by the Greek theology of necessity or fate) but in the free fall of finite spirit (the Adamic myth).[13] This is the 'profoundly speculative' feature of the story of the fall, which in 1831 is transferred from Part III of the lectures, where it was earlier discussed in relation to Christianity,[14] to Part II and the Jewish religion (pp. 740-741).

Judaism gains by thus having its myth of creation and fall returned to it rather than being expropriated to the framework of Christian theology, as it was in Hegel's earlier lectures. But there is a complicating factor at work here as well. Hegel argues that the 'story of the fall lay fallow in Jewish religion and attained its true meaning only in the Christian religion'. To be sure, the struggle between good and evil does constitute an essential feature of Jewish religion; this is especially striking in the Psalms of David, where 'anguish cries aloud from the innermost depths of the soul in the consciousness of its sinfulness, followed by the most anguished plea for forgiveness and reconciliation'. But this depth of anguish is known only as pertaining to the single individual in contingent fashion rather than as an eternal moment of spirit, and it finally remains unresolved in Judaism (pp. 741-742).

Related to this, in Hegel's view, is the fact that the laws of God as revealed to the Jewish people are not laws of freedom. They are not given by reason but prescribed by God - all of them, ranging from the most petty cultic regulations to the universal ethical foundations of human existence. The vocation of the Jewish people is to give itself up wholly to the service of the Lord, which accounts for their 'admirable steadfastness', but which also means that 'there is no freedom vis-à-vis this firm bond'. The Lord finally does not enter into the human combat with evil but simply punishes evil. The finite subject engages in an unresolved struggle between good and evil, resulting in contrition and anguish, from which there is no liberation. There can be a liberation only if the struggle and anguish are taken into the divine life itself (pp. 683-685n).

These critical remarks are accounted for in part by the hermeneutical and political context of the 1831 lectures. We know that, as a result of recent events, in 1830-1831 Hegel had become deeply concerned with the relationship between religion and state and especially with the task of creating and preserving free political institutions.[15] Only a free religion can serve as the foundation of a free state. In this respect Judaism is found wanting. It is on the way to freedom but has not arrived at its ethical actualization. Hegel has now taken up the other perspective to which I referred when analysing the advance from Greek to Jewish religion in 1827. From the point of view of monotheism and spiritual subjectivity, Judaism is higher; but from the point of view of divine-human mediation and free ethical institutions, Greek religion is higher.

This latter perspective pervades the 1831 lectures, which combine an emancipatory, world-transforming motif with a dialectically related one, namely, the self-mediation of the triune God, a mediation that is both internal and external, both within the divine life and constitutive of worldly activity. In this respect, too, Judaism is found wanting. The God of Israel is not an 'inwardly developing' God; God does not take the anguish of the world into and upon himself, nor is he engaged in the human socio-political and cultural struggles for freedom. This requires, Hegel thought, another step in religious consciousness, anticipated by the figure of the phoenix and the myths of Adonis and Osiris, but fulfilled in the death of God on the cross of Christ.

VI Concluding Observations

The Jews, however, have also experienced a death of God: they experienced it in the death camps of Auschwitz,[16] and they experienced approximations of it earlier in the pogroms, the crusades, the revolt of Bar-Kochba, the destruction of the second temple, the Babylonian captivity. They have learned, as Emil Fackenheim said,[17] that the command of Auschwitz was precisely **not** to deny God, not to hand Hitler a posthumous victory through the destruction of Judaism; thus they arose from the ashes, and the nation of Israel was reborn.

Hegel underestimated the inner resources of Judaism - its profound spirituality, its sublime vision of God, its indestructible faith, its poetic eloquence - even as he glimpsed these qualities and even as his portrayal of Judaism underwent a significant metamorphosis. He was unable finally to transcend the inherited posture of Christian superiority, and this, very simply, was the root of his ambivalence. Judaism **must** remain for Christians a 'dark riddle' so long as they retain the conviction that the old Israel is superseded by the new. For what appears to be distinctively true and final about Christianity is those very beliefs wherein it claims to surpass Judaism - the triune God, the incarnation of the Word of God, the primacy of gospel over law, the universal availability of redemption, etc. It is indeed difficult for Christians to acknowledge the relativity of these beliefs. Yet the truth that emerges from Hegel's long struggle with Judaism, and indeed with the history of religion as a whole, is that every exclusive claim to religious finality is parochial and not rationally sustainable. No single religion is **the** consummate religion; rather the great world religions share in and contribute to the consummation of religion in quite unique, but perhaps also strangely convergent, ways. Hegel, I think, knew this without quite recognizing it; what he offers in *Determinate Religion* is not so much a developmental history of religion as a typology of distinctive shapes of religious consciousness, each of which displays its distinctive contributions and limits.[18] Christianity is, to be sure, exempted from this relativization, and Hegel's inconsistency at this point must, in the light of what is called postmodernity, be firmly rejected.[19] But in the case of Christianity, as well as other religions, a recognition of the relativity and plurality of religions need not entail an abandonment of one's own faith; rather it can provide the occasion for its deepening and enrichment - an affirmation that we do indeed know the absolute but only in a plurality of mutually transformative ways.

Notes

1. Published in *History and System: Hegel's Philosophy of History*, ed. Robert L. Perkins, State University of New York Press, Albany, 1984, pp. 47-63.

2. G.W.F. Hegel, *Early Theological Writings*, trans. T.M. Knox, University of Chicago Press, 1984, pp. 68-69, 98-99, 177, 181, 190-191, 298.

3. Ibid., pp. 158-159.

4. *HPR*, §§209, 210; see Avineri, 'The Fossil and the Phoenix', pp. 54, 61n.

5. Avineri, 'The Fossil and The Phoenix', pp. 51-54.

6. Ibid., pp. 55-61.

7. The first edition was published by Eduard Gans in 1837 and based primarily on materials from 1830-31. On this occasion, however, Hegel limited the lectures to the Introduction and Part I, the Oriental World, which included the first of the two sections in which Judaism is discussed. For the subsequent parts we must assume that Gans drew his materials from the latest lectures in which they were discussed, those of 1828-29 and possibly 1826-27. Karl Hegel issued a second edition in 1840 (translated into English by J. Sibree in 1857), in which he supplemented Gans's text primarily with manuscripts from his father's own hand; but Hegel's lecture manuscript of 1830-31 breaks off before 'the end of the Introduction, and Karl Hegel's revisions appear to focus on the Introduction, which is greatly expanded in the second edition. A comparison of the two sections on Judaism (*PH*, pp. 195-198, 321-323) with the philosophy of religion lectures of 1827 and 1831 makes it virtually certain that the philosophy of history material postdates 1827. Despite the more recent editorial efforts of Lasson and Hoffmeister (to which Avineri does not refer), a new critical edition of the lectures on the philosophy of world history is badly needed.

8. G.W.F. Hegel, *Vorlesungen über die Philosophie der Religion*, ed. Walter Jaeschke, 3 vols, Felix Meiner Verlag, Hamburg, 1983-1985; *Lectures on the Philosophy of Religion*, 3 vols, ed. Peter C. Hodgson, trans. R.F. Brown, P.C. Hodgson, J.M. Stewart, University of California Press, Berkeley, Los Angeles, London, 1984-1987. Portions of this article are based on materials contained in my editorial introduction to vol. 2 of the English edition, *Determinate Religion*, scheduled for publication in the fall or winter of 1987; the use of these

materials is with the permission of the publisher. Page citations in the text are to this edition.

9. Emil L. Fackenheim, 'Hegel and Judaism: A Flaw in the Hegelian Mediation', in *The Legacy of Hegel: Proceedings of the Marquette Symposium,* ed. J.J. O'Malley et al., Martinus Nijhoff, The Hague, 1973, pp. 161-162.

10. The place of Judaism in the *Phenomenology of Spirit* has been much debated but never satisfactorily resolved. Brief allusions to it may be found in the section on the 'unhappy consciousness' - for example, the reference to 'the alien essence' that 'condemns singularity' (PS, p. 128) - and in the view of most interpreters that is the extent of it. But Walter Jaeschke has recently argued that Hegel's discussion of 'the light-essence' (*das Lichtwesen*) as the first form of 'natural religion' (pp. 418-420) is not a reference to Persian religion, as generally thought, but to the God of Israel. He attempts to establish this by identifying numerous similarities between this brief section of the *Phenomenology* and the treatment of the idea of God in Jewish religion in the 1821 lecture manuscript, where, for example, the sublimity of God is also defined in terms of the metaphor of 'light' - the God who creates by the word that is pure light and who covers himself 'with light as with a garment' (LPR, vol. 2, p. 136). See Walter Jaeschke, *Die Vernunft in der Religion: Studien zur Grundlegung der spekulativen Religionsphilosophie,* Inaugural dissertation, Ruhr-Universität Bochum, 1985, pp. 288-295.

11. Reinhard Leuze, *Die außerchristlichen Religionen bei Hegel,* Vandenhoeck & Ruprecht, Göttingen, 1975, pp. 170 ff.

12. See LPR, vol. 1, pp. 7-8.

13. I have appropriated Paul Ricoeur's categories here (*The Symbolism of Evil,* trans. Emerson Buchanan, Beacon Press, Boston, 1967, pp. 306-346), but they fit Hegel's analysis nicely.

14. LPR, vol. 3, pp. 104-108, 207-211, 300-304.

15. See Walter Jaeschke, 'Hegel's Last Year in Berlin', in *Hegel's Philosophy of Action,* ed. Lawrence S. Stepelevich and David Lamb, Humanities Press, Atlantic Highlands, NJ, 1983, pp. 31-48. See also Hegel's discussion of the relationship of religion to the state at the end of Part I of the 1831 lectures (LPR, vol. 1, pp. 451-460).

16. Elie Wiesel, *Night,* Avon Books, New York, 1969, p. 76: '"Where is God now?" ... "Where is He? Here He is - He is hanging here on this gallows" '.

17. Emil Fackenheim, *God's Presence in History: Jewish Affirmations and Philosophical Reflections,* New York University Press, New York, 1970, chapter 3.

18. See Walter Jaeschke, 'Zur Logik der Bestimmten Religion', in *Hegels Logik der Philosophie: Religion und Philosophie in der Theorie des absoluten Geistes,* ed. Dieter Henrich and Rolf-Peter Horstmann, Frommann-Holzboog Verlag, Stuttgart, 1984, pp. 172-188. I also discuss this matter at the conclusion of my introduction to *Determinate Religion.*

19. What relativizes Christianity for Hegel is its relation not to other religions but to the absolute philosophy. But philosophical truth is as relative as religious truth; and one can argue, as R.G.R. Mure does, that Hegelianism 'knows as a conclusion from its own premises that it is itself a thesis which must beget its own antithesis' (A *Study of Hegel's Logic,* Clarendon Press, Oxford, 1950, p. 327).

6 Commitments to Time in Reformation Protestant Theology, Hegelian Idealism, and Marxism

ROBERT PATTMAN

This essay addresses Reformation Protestant theology, Hegelian idealism, and Marxism as **theoretical practices** which exemplify commitments to time, and it seeks the expression of these commitments in their respective contents (theoretical products). Thus it analyses **how** these theoretical systems conceptualize social phenomena and **what** the conceptualized social phenomena are. It attempts to derive from Reformation Protestantism the Hegelian and ultimately the Marxist commitments to time.

I

Reformation Protestantism locates movement in a God, and the idea of a moving temporal God is ideally developed in Luther's struggle as a Catholic monk. Luther regularly confessed his sins yet experienced no change. After confession he was still a sinner, still tormented by desires of the flesh. Indeed confession perpetuated his sins: confessing to God his lack of humility, he gained pride for which he confessed, and so on. He was in despair. How could he, a sinner, relate to God? The recognition of his desperate condition - like the recognition by an addict of his addiction - was, however, an essential stage in his quest for freedom - freedom from his addiction to the regularity of confession. The conception of good underlying confession as the exchangeable opposite of evil was experienced despairingly by Luther as a nominal or indifferent opposite, yet this implied the possibility of good as an experiential opposite. Luther resolved his despair, became a Protestant as it were, by articulating good as absolute Being (God) and as absolute in virtue of relating to evil or saving individuals.

Luther describes the good or godly individual as 'always a sinner, always repentant, always righteous'.[1] This is not a justification of the regularity of confession, but, on the contrary, a critique of the mechanical process whereby the individual is filled up with good like petrol and filled up again when it runs out. For Luther the good individual is always in the process of becoming good, his becoming 'lying midway between two contraries',[2] between God and the temptation to deify self, to perceive morality as the consequence of worldly or individuals' works.

Becoming good is represented in Reformation Protestantism as the renunciation of self and the present through faith, i.e. through believing one's becoming or one's be-ing to be not one's own but God's. 'I must throw away (my own) person', writes Luther.[3] Faith in this sense does not imply an immediate and voyeuristic rejection of worldly reality. It is an explicit practice or process continually addressing worldly reality in order to transcend it. The faithful, Calvin writes, 'must accustom themselves to such a contempt of the present life as nowise engenders any hatred of it'.[4] Through faith the eternity of becoming and the future is rooted in the continuity of the self and the present.

Knowledge of God through the theoretical practice of faith 'rests satisfied', writes Calvin, 'with the image in the mirror'.[5] To see God directly is to be God-like, which presupposes stasis. Calvin compares the faithful to prisoners 'bound with terrestrial and corporeal fetters'[6] but illuminated by the dim light from the small cell window – the dim light, the revelation of God's mercy. To distinguish God as 'he' ultimately is, the opposite of the temporal world (stasis), from God as 'his' activity, as he appears to the faithful, Reformation Protestantism distinguishes God from Christ, the individual God-man or mediator. The problem of how sensuous man experiences God was resolved for Luther by articulating God as saviour through Christ, or Christ as 'a ladder let down by the Father to bring us up to himself'.[7] The qualitative transforming work of faith is the mediating movement of God through Christ. **Becoming** through faith is **be-ing** Christ. 'Faith', writes Luther, 'makes of you and of Christ as it were one person, so that you cannot be divided from Christ, but cling to him, as though you were called Christ'.[8]

Christ's death marked, for Luther, the beginning of the possibility of mediation between God and sensuous man, the past and the present. For his death was not merely sensuous death and hence oblivion, but a sensuous sacrifice through which he realized his divine nature, continuing to exist but as purely divine. Sensuous man could recollect Christ's sacrifice because it was sensuous, but mere (sensuous) recollection could not constitute the basis, according to Luther, of a relationship with the divine; the divine was continually existing or present-centred, not a life in the past. Luther repudiated the exegesis of the Eucharist and of Christ's invocation 'Do this in remembrance of Me' which 'made man and his "remembrance" the cause of Christ's presence in the Sacrament'.[9] Luther's exegesis was 'Christocentric' rather than 'anthropocentric', taking 'as its point of departure not the present, in which believers did the remembering, but the past, in which they remembered',[10] relating to the past not as a moment of (past) chronological time but as an eternal present - an eternal tension between divine and sensuous mediating the sensuous present, mediating remembrance.

To recall Christ's self-sacrifice, according to Luther, was to recall that Christ had done so once for all at the end of the age to put away sin.[11] Luther condemned the notion that individuals could receive 'the forgiveness of sins through their sacrifice',[12] through the repetition (and hence the mere ritual) of self-invented deeds of piety such as fasting, etc. This was self-deification or pride - the very sin for which Christ sacrificed himself. Christ, Luther explained, was 'the sacrifice which God Himself has appointed and with which God is pleased. . . . Because God Himself has appointed this sacrifice, we should have no doubt that this sacrifice completely accomplished everything it was intended to accomplish'.[13] To recall Christ's self-sacrifice without re-enacting or repeating it was to allow the present to be mediated by a unique historical event (as opposed to relating the present to mere past). Mediated by the past, the present itself becomes a unique event rather than a mere temporal and repeatable moment. 'Since the death of Christ and until the end of this world', writes Luther, 'no sacrifice can avail any longer except the sacrifice of praise', i.e., praise through faith in Christ the mediator, the redeemer.

The practice of faith distinguishes two modes of temporality: (1) that in which the present is synonymous with the immediate and the movement from past to present to future is chronological or quantitative; and (2) that in which the present is the initiator, the imposer of time, and movement from past to present to future is the consequence of activity and therefore qualitative. The Reformation Protestant exemplifies, through faith, a commitment to the latter mode of temporality while not rejecting, but on the contrary upholding the former as worldly, sensuous temporality. His critique is directed at the temptation to apply worldly temporality to divine activity, to make the grace of God consequent on the chronological and therefore mechanical and ritualistic works of individuals.

The Church, for Luther, was situated in the worldly, chronological realm, the realm of perception, and at the same time transcended this realm, for it was nothing other than those engaged in a reciprocally active communion with God - a communion which occurred in time but in which the individual, through Christ, participated in eternity. Participating in eternity or the transcendental did not imply timelessness for it was an eternal process of transcending the realm of perception. Or put differently, it was a critique of the eternal temptation to collapse the transcendental level into the worldly, chronological and perceptual level, the true Church (the 'community of believers') into its institutional framework. To succumb to this temptation was to deny qualitative mediating activity and time, to substitute Christ as mediator for the immediate perceptual reality of the **human** preacher. The deification of the perceptual reality of the Church and its preachers was characterized, as Luther saw it, in Catholicism. The Catholic preacher, a holy shepherd in relation to his passive flock, had a monopoly of divine power, magically or immediately mediating the temporal and the transcendental. For Luther - the practitioner - explicitly committed to time, the struggle to save souls did not require the submission of man to man, but of man to God. The struggle to save souls in Luther's preaching was a struggle intended to inspire struggle by those to whom he preached, to make God **present** for them by actively and continuously, through faith, seeking him.

Since the commitment in Reformation Protestantism to mediating or qualitative time as divine sustains and presupposes chronological or quantitative time as worldly, Reformation Protestantism justified, as the good worldly life, the subordination of activity or labour to time. The worldly or natural life of the individual was compared with the running out of an hourglass, and the individual was implored never to indulge himself, to be idle, to waste time. 'The good life', wrote Luther, 'consists of never standing still'.[14]

II

This essay interprets Hegelianism and Marxism as responding to an **idealistic** yearning in Reformation Protestantism for mediating or qualitative time, as attempting to exemplify mediating or qualitative time as - rather than preserving it (as divine) from - the temporality of the sensuous worldly individual. Hegelianism and Marxism are conceived as addressing the problem of how to express Be-ing or qualitative movement as absolute without making it divine, that is without making it the movement of an ultimately static and therefore inaccessible Being.

Hegel articulates this contradiction characterizing Reformation Protestantism between Be-ing (or God's activity through Christ) and Being (or God), in his critique of the 'representational consciousness' of 'revealed religion' (i.e. Reformation Protestantism). In religion, Being is inaccessible or external and therefore has to be re-presented in the present. Reformation Protestantism comprehends this necessity as the necessity of God's representation (in Christ) as a sensuous individual; and, through faith in God's necessary representation, experiences Being in the present as Be-ing, or qualitative, mediating movement.

Yet the moments of God's self-revelation in 'revealed religion' - his transcendence or Being and his immediacy or presence or Be-ing - are divided into temporally successive moments, his immediacy manifested in his life as a human individual and his transcendence in the resurrection after death. Hegel articulates mediation not from the point of view of a contrived mediator, an individual God-man who

105

mediates (the faithful), but from the point of view of mediation itself, in which the transcendental and immediate nature of absolute Being are thought simultaneously. Hegel criticizes Reformation Protestantism for 'tracing back'[15] (chronologically) to get to absolute Being, for seeking the origins of mediation outside mediation. Reformation Protestantism is a critique of the immediate recollection of Christ which obscures his role as mediator by retrieving a purely chronological past, yet, paradoxically, immediately recollects the origins of mediation. This is apparent, for example, in Milton's narrative-like account in 'Paradise Lost' of the beginning of the possibility of mediation or a qualitatively active relationship between individual and God. At first there is only heaven, then with Satan's revolt and expulsion from heaven there is hell; then there is man who knows 'good by itself, and evil not at all';[16] then with the Fall and expulsion from man's original state of Paradise - Eden - there is man who knows 'both good and evil, good lost and evil got';[17] then there is Christ the mediator who activates the difference between good and evil. Goodness is no longer equated with Eden, with an accidental physical state, but is transformed into the necessary other of evil, to be reached not immediately but through a process of struggle. At first, therefore, there is stasis, followed (with the Fall) by its immediate opposite, quantitative activity and time (Adam recognizes its quantitative nature when he asks despairingly just after the Fall, 'Why is life giv'n to be thus wrested from us?'[18]); which in turn is followed by the possibility of qualitative activity and time. Mediation is contrived in Reformation Protestantism in the sense of being thought of after the beginning of human history. Qualitative or mediating history is, for the Reformation Protestant, redemptive history - possible only after man has already 'fallen', i.e. during quantitative or 'natural' history.

For Hegel there is nothing beyond or prior to mediating activity so that it is not contrived in order to differentiate or relate already fragmented or immediate opposites (God and the worldly individual). It is therefore the originator and imposer of human history and time and not a different - divine - mode of temporality. For Hegel the self-mediated individual, rather than the divine which mediates individuals, is absolute. Whereas divine mediation implies self-consciousness through (blind) faith, self-mediation is self-consciousness. Hegel argues that the 'community of believers' - the faithful - is not yet aware that its consciousness of God as self-conscious in Jesus Christ is its own self-consciousness. For Hegel, to be self-conscious is to identify self-consciousness and consciousness of absolute Being.

How, for Hegel, does self-mediating or conscious activity impose time and history? What is the nature of this activity which, for Hegel, is the essential, definitive characteristic of man? In his *Introduction to the Reading of Hegel*, Kojève expresses it as movement which is engendered in the future and which arises from human desire: 'that is', Kojève explains, 'desire that is directed toward an entity that does not exist and has not existed in the real natural world'.[19] Kojève distinguishes the Hegelian notion of human time (the consequence of conscious activity), in which future takes primacy, from 'biological time' dictated by the past, distinguishing the conscious human 'project' from action as a given and immediate response to given stimuli. This is not to suggest that the past has no place in Hegel's notion of human time. On the contrary, 'the past', for Hegel, is what distinguishes the 'project', as Kojève explains, from a simple 'dream' or 'utopia'.[20] The movement engendered in the future does not relate immediately to the present via the past, for the present is a human construction - the culmination of past constructive activity.

Conscious activity, as Hegel understands it, brings about 'essential changes'. Essential changes constitute, for Hegel, human time, not the regular movement from one mathematical or quantitative unit to another. Human time for Hegel is a conceptual as opposed to a temporal phenomenon, conscious activity or movement itself rather than something external which moves. To comprehend human time purely temporally - as chronology - is to conceive human activity as essentially repetitious (subject to the regularity of quantitative movement). Hegel defines human time as 'the Concept itself which is there in empirical existence',[21] i.e. in the natural sensuous world. The difference which Hegel articulates between a conceptual and a temporal understanding of human time is analogous to the difference between watching a film as three-dimensional images on a screen and watching it as a succession of still frames on a rotating spool. Each moving frame is simultaneously a 'now' and not a 'now', a point but a point lost in time. For a particular frame makes no particular impression on time, prolonging it as much as any other frame. The sustainable reality is not, thus, 'now' but 'nowness' or still space divided from quantitative time. By contrast the movement of the projected film - the relationship between the three-dimensional images on the screen - is necessary not mechanical, qualitative not quantitative, intrinsic not external. The present is not divided from past and future as a quantitative moment but brings about past and future by (using Hegelian terminology) 'negating' itself. Movement or temporality in the film as seen on the screen is located in space, and space is transformed by temporality.

Conceptual thinking implies consciousness of the unity of space and time. Time which is the Concept itself 'in empirical existence' has, Hegel explains, 'a real existence through space' and 'space is first truly differentiated by time'.[22] Time and space conceived in isolation are abstractions - 'nowness' or 'hereness', 'the immediate existence of quantity'.[23] Quantity or 'magnitude' is conceived by Hegel as an 'unessential distinction' or relation - an abstract difference (between 'nows' and 'heres'). Quantifiable or mathematical objects are dead: 'we can stop at any one of them', writes Hegel; 'the next one starts afresh on its own account without the first having moved itself on to the next, and without any necessary connection arising through the nature of the thing itself'.[24] A mathematical conception of human life - like seeing the film as still frames on a rotating spool instead of as three-dimensional intrinsically temporal images - can not comprehend the unique qualitative nature of the present as it differentiates itself from or relates to past and future through 'self-negation'. Severing time from space, it makes time external in relation to human life, equalizing 'nows' as 'nowness'.

Like Reformation Protestantism, Hegelianism is a critique of the conception of immediate or quantitative time and space as the absolute temporal and spatial mode of human existence. Whereas Reformation Protestantism (through faith in the absolute) distinguishes immediate and absolute as two separate spheres of reality - the worldly temporal (quantitative) and the transcendental temporal (qualitative) - Hegel seeks to unite immediate and absolute as the only sphere of reality. Hegel derives from the appearance of immediate time and space (as human time and space) the unity of time and space. He ' moves' from the illusion (as he conceives it) of the absolute existence of temporally conceived 'nows' and spatially conceived 'heres' to abstract time and space (i.e. to consciousness of the illusion). Temporally conceived 'nows' and spatially conceived 'heres', Hegel explains, 'interrupt' time and space but merely exist in relation to each other - time and space as such 'absolutely uninterrupted thereby'.[25] He then 'moves' to 'nows' and 'heres' as absolute, qualitative and unique, as 'self-differentiating', exemplified in his conscious activity, his theoretical practice.

The fragmentation of human time and space - the conception of time and space as quantitative mediums - is illusory for Hegel in the sense that it is a fragmentation in Thought. Consciousness of this conception as illusory, as the product of the fragmentation of Thought and spatial/temporal Being in Thought implies not only the (self-conscious Hegelian) theorist who exemplifies a unity of Thought and Being, but also an original unity of Thought and Being in Thought.

Unlike the 'original unity', in Reformation Protestant theology, of God and the individual in Eden, the original unity of Thought and Being is not separated chronologically vis-à-vis the 'Fall' and quantitative chronological history from the possibility of qualitative history. Rather, Hegel seeks the possibility of qualitative history within the unity of Thought and Being, articulating Thought as imposing or causing time and history.

For Hegel, human history refers to the self-development of Thought - a process towards the reconciliation and transcendence of fragmented Thought and Being in Thought. The comprehension, as Hegel sees it, of the unity of Thought and Being through Christ ('revealed religion' or Reformation Protestantism) represents, for Hegel, a final stage in the self-development of Thought culminating in the unity of Thought and Being in Thought itself (Hegelianism). Self-conscious Thought (Hegelianism) reflects upon history not as a quantifiable medium to which it is subject. Time 'appears as Thought's destiny and necessity', Hegel explains, 'where Thought is not yet complete within itself',[26] where 'Thought' is still developing.

But since the 'completion' of Thought is the culmination of history, how can completed or self-conscious Thought impose temporality and continue human history? Unlike Reformation Protestantism which perpetuates qualitative (redemptive) history through faith by making the future restoration of the original unity of God and the individual a possibility with death, the Hegelian theorist exemplifying the unity of Thought and Being in the present marks the end of history. Ironically, the attempt in Hegelianism to develop and exemplify human time as conscious movement - movement engendered in the future - succeeds in denying the possibility of future time and history. The implicit original unity of Thought and Being presupposed by the Hegelian theorist is as static and idealistic as the unity of God and the individual in Eden. How Thought and Being become fragmented is as problematic as the Fall from Eden. History is sandwiched, as it were, between an implicit unity of Thought and Being and an exemplifier of this unity - the Hegelian theorist. For Hegel, man is an ideal prior to history causing history through self-fragmentation, and realizing himself by becoming conscious of having caused (though not causing) history.

Ironically, Hegel responds critically to the contradiction in Reformation Protestant theology between qualitative, mediating time and timelessness, yet reproduces this contradiction in an even more explicit form. Indeed Hegelianism has been interpreted, on the one hand, as denying the existence of time and on the other as accounting for time and history. For example, MacTaggart argues that Thought, as Hegel conceives it, exists 'eternally in its full perfection', so that its development is 'reconstruction and not construction';[27] so that time and history do not really occur. Brinkley, however, argues that the idea of an implicit unity of Thought and Being in Hegelianism grounds the possibility of time and history. For the goal or dynamic of history, according to Brinkley's interpretation of Hegelianism, is the recovery of the original unity, the implicit beginning, 'the attempt to overcome the very detachment which made history possible'.[28] According to Brinkley's interpretation, then, Hegel does not reconstruct or recover the original implicit and therefore static unity of Thought and Being, but on the contrary, recognizes this as an unrecoverable ideal. In this sense, recognition or consciousness is creative rather than repetitive - creating the meaning of the unity of Thought and Being rather than simply reproducing the meaning of the unity already there - the implicit unity. Consciousness is creative, according to Brinkley, in virtue of orienting itself towards this implicit unity as an ideal.

III

Marx responds to Hegelianism as a contradictory theoretical system, focusing not exclusively upon the qualitative temporality or the timelessness of the Hegelian 'Concept' or 'Thought'. Thus Marx interprets the Hegelian self-conscious Concept as having revolutionary **and** quietistic implications. He praises Hegel for grasping 'the self-creation of man as a process',[29] as qualitative or essential change **and** criticizes him for conceiving essential change as change in consciousness, i.e. as change only in the interpretation of reality. (Marx likened the 'Young Hegelians' who demanded freedom from the illusions of consciousness as an end in itself to someone 'who had the idea that men were drowned in water because they were possessed with the idea of gravity'.[30])

In criticizing this sense of change as change in consciousness, Marx is criticizing Hegel for failing to uphold man as the bearer or subject of 'the self-creation of man'. For Hegel identifies, as Marx explains, 'the absolute subject **as a process**' (my emphasis), the 'existent' Concept as time, failing to differentiate subject as author of the process from the process itself, except as a transcendental and static (implicit) unity of subject and object, Thought and Being. This process comprises: (1) the 'subject alienating itself' by objectifying itself, i.e. by dividing itself (as Thought) from the immediate and objective spatio-temporal world, dividing the transcendental from the quantitative or mathematical; and (2) 'returning from alienation into itself' in virtue of being conscious of this division as its own creation, thus 'retracting this alienation into itself and the subject as this process'. Marx characterizes this process as 'a pure restless revolving within itself'.[31] With regard to the objective world in which man lives - the world of Being - there is no change. For the retraction or 'appropriation of man's objectified and estranged essential powers', as Marx explains, 'is only an appropriation which takes place in consciousness, in pure thought'.[32]

While Hegel conceives 'objective man . . . as the result of his own labour . . . which is at first only possible in the form of estrangement',[33] he nevertheless preserves the 'estranged moment' - the appearance of an independent and external objective world, the appearance of independent and external time and space. Like Reformation Protestantism, Hegelianism needs the imposition of object upon subject, time (as chronology) upon man, in order to distinguish from it qualitative or mediating time. Reformation Protestantism exemplifies the latter through faith, i.e. by assigning it to a different (divine) sphere of reality; it is consciousness of the division between absolute subject and natural or quantitative Being (this division occurring as a result of the 'Fall'), re-establishing and perpetuating it as a division between conscious or qualitative movement as transcendental and quantitative or natural Being. Hegel, by contrast, re-establishes this division as a unity within the absolute Subject - Thought - perpetuating the imposition of object upon subject, time upon man as a necessary illusion.

Hegel identifies consciousness as the individual's capacity to think relationally (from the viewpoint not of an independent static subject but of the relationship of subject and object), and this, for Hegel, is consciousness of objectification as alienation, or self-consciousness. Marx develops Hegel's relational conception of subject and object without treating subject as process or Thought itself and object as appearance as such. The subject differentiates himself from the object - is conscious - for Hegel, in virtue of being self-conscious, already conscious; and for Marx, in virtue of being an objective being. Unlike the infinitely revolving abstract Spirit, objective Being is not merely mediating but, in Mészaros's words, a 'self-mediating being of nature'.[34] It creates and establishes only objects, Marx writes, 'because it is established by objects, because it is fundamentally nature'.[35] It does not preserve creative time (as infinitely circular, divine or human) from natural time (as finitely linear, as quantitative or chronological), but realizes it as the temporality imposed in its creative, progressive self-mediating relationship with nature. In this sense time changes, but not purely quantitatively, not indifferently to human activity. Time has to change in order to be realized, and, like Hegel, Marx seeks change **within** time not outside time (as a static chronological scale). But whereas Hegel (and Luther) idealistically preserve change **within** time from change **in** time (articulating the latter as change from without) Marx realizes change within time as change in time.

Pure or abstract Thought identifying alienation and objectification supersedes history as such, articulating change as change within the present, change within itself, externalizing the alienated present. Marx distinguishes alienation from objectification - the former an historical and historically supersedable form of the latter. As an historical subject, he addresses his opposite as a real historical appearance without identifying it as really himself (as extra-historical abstract Thought). The Marxist analysis does not perpetuate the object of its critique by failing to sustain it, but, as mediating subject and object, exemplifies as a (practically) realizable possibility unalienated society. Or put differently, it exemplifies as a possibility time and history beyond alienation.

The possibility of unalienated society is derived historically by Marx from the present - capitalist society. Capitalism separates or alienates the individual from his labour, transforming the individual into an abstract possessor of an exchangeable commodity - 'labour power'. As a commodity, his labour does not impose temporality, but, on the contrary, is subject to time as chronology. Time becomes an abstract amount or quantity to be filled with labour power - the amount of labour power expended - 'labour time'. Filling time, 'labour power' objectifies itself repetitively, for there is no change in labour with respect to purely chronological change. Indeed purely chronological time continues when work has ceased, as 'lost' time, or time not expended by 'labour power'.

In relation to 'labour power', the alienated individual possessor is timeless, unable to realize himself existentially. Objectification, in capitalism, becomes a mere and repetitive means towards this fleeting timeless end. Unmediated by the timeless possessor, it immediately fulfils the individual's desire for self-realization. It is animalic - dictated by the past, not engendered in the future. Addressing and sustaining capitalism as a real objective society, Marx presupposes the possibility of socialist society, as a real objective being-oriented or self-conscious as opposed to individual (possessor)-oriented society.

Marx interprets Hegel as expressing the alienation, the imposition of capitalist labour or objectification, idealizing, however, the individual as self-conscious as essence, and reconciling him to the alienated appearance of himself as abstract ego or possessor. Being, for Hegel, realizes itself (as Thought) in virtue of being conscious of not being abstract ego, revealing the latter as its estranged appearance. For Marx, the Hegelian concept of 'estrangement as nothing but estrangement of self-consciousness'[36] highlights the impotence of the abstract ego to effect real change, its enslavement to capitalist labour.

This is apparent in Hegel's conception of the 'Master-Slave' relationship, in which the 'Slave', recognizing the 'Master' as the product of his (the Slave's) labour, negates in his mind the immediate imposition of the 'Master', of externally imposed, possession-oriented work. The 'Slave' is really master of the 'Master' in virtue of mediating him (as real appearance of Master), in virtue of being self-conscious, of recognizing himself as producer. Idealizing the abstract ego as self-creative, Hegel expresses it as fulfilling the essentially human desire for self-realization or 'recognition' by negating animalic or immediately fulfilling desire as its real and necessary appearance. For Hegel human time, time engendered in the future arises from the human or mediated desire of the Slave in opposition to the animalic or immediate desire of the Master. As Kojève writes, concerning Hegel, 'the Desire for Recognition . . . - by opposing the Master to the Slave - engenders History and moves it (as long as it is not definitively overcome by Satisfaction)',[37] i.e. through the immediate negation of the Master.

The objective sensuous world as described in Reformation Protestantism also epitomizes capitalism or possession-oriented society. The temptation inherent in objective sensuous reality to encroach upon divine reality is the temptation inherent in possessions to assume the role of Master as opposed to Slave, possessor as opposed to possession. Whereas Hegelianism idealizes the Slave or possession, Reformation Protestantism idealizes the Master or possessor. Thus Calvin describes God as a possessor: 'God', he writes, 'trains, persuades, moderates our heart and governs it as his **possession**'[38] (emphasis mine). To assume the role of possessor was to deny the omnipotence of God. Reformation Protestantism thus described and legitimized the transformation of the individual in capitalism into possession - 'labour power' - imploring the individual to work as an end in itself rather than as a means to possess, to resist the temptation inherent in possessions of idleness and hedonism (wasting time).

Marx accused 'the philosophers' of having only 'interpreted the world in various ways'. For Marx, 'the point is to change it'.[39] In interpreting the imposition of time upon human activity (as 'labour power') in capitalism, Hegelianism and Reformation Protestantism legitimized it, yet simultaneously pointed beyond it, by exemplifying commitments to qualitative or creative time and activity.

Notes

1. *Reformation Writings of Martin Luther* [RWML], trans. from the Weimar edition by B.L. Woolf, Lutterworth Press, London, 1952- , vol. 56, p. 442.

2. RWML , vol. 12, p. 559.

3. Luther, *Bondage of the Will,* p. 207.

4. Calvin, *Institutes of the Christian Religion,* trans. Henry Beveridge, Calvin Translation Society, Edinburgh, 1845, Book III, Chapter 9, §1.

5. Ibid., Book I.

6. Ibid., Book I.

7. Quoted in E.A. Wood, *Captive to the Word,* 1969, p. 186.

8. RWML, vol. 40, p. 285.

9. Pelikan, Jaroslav, *Luther the Expositor: Introduction to the Reformer's Exegetical Writings,* Concordia Publishing House, Saint Louis, Mo., 1969, p. 217.

10. Ibid., p: 217.

11. Luther, 'Lectures on Hebrews', in RWML, vol. 57, pp. 217-218.

12. Luther, 'Sermon on Hebrews 8:3', in RWML, vol. 45, p. 397.

13. RWML, vol. 52, p. 229.

14. RWML, vol. 40, p. 526.

15. PS, p. 463.

16. Milton, J., *Paradise Lost,* New American Library, New York, 1968, Book XI, line 89.

17. Ibid., Book IX, line 1072.

18. Ibid., Book XI, lines 502-3.

19. Kojève, Alexandre, *Introduction to the Reading of Hegel,* ed. A. Bloom, Cornell University Press, Ithaca and London, 1980, p. 134.

20. Ibid., p. 137.

21. 'Die Zeit ist der Begriff selbst, der da ist', Hegel, *Phänomenologie des Geistes,* ed. J. Hoffmeister, Meiner, Hamburg, 1952, p. 9. Kojève (*Introduction to the Reading of Hegel,* p. 101) translates this as 'Time is the Concept itself, which is there in empirical existence'. See *PS,* p. 27.

22. *HPN,* p. 43.

23. *HPN,* p. 43.

24. *PS,* p. 26.

25. *HPN,* p. 29.

26. *PS,* p. 487.

27. MacTaggart, J., *Studies in the Hegelian Dialectic,* Cambridge University Press, 1896, p. 160.

28. Brinkley, Alan B., 'Time in Hegel's Phenomenology', in *Studies in Hegel. Tulane Studies in Philosophy, vol. IX,* Tulane University, New Orleans, and Martinus Nijhoff, The Hague, 1960.

29. Marx, K., *Paris Manuscripts,* Progress Publishers, Moscow, 1977, p. 140.

30. Marx, K., *The German Ideology,* Lawrence and Wishart, London, 1974, p. 37.

31. Marx, *Paris Manuscripts,* Progress Publishers, Moscow, 1977, p. 152.

32. Ibid., p. 139.

33. Ibid., p. 140.

34. Mészáros, I., *Marx's Theory of Alienation,* Merlin Press, London, 1978.

35. Marx, *Paris Manuscripts,* Progress Publishers, Moscow, 1977, p. 144.

36. Ibid., p. 142.

37. Kojève, *An Introduction to the Reading of Hegel*, p. 135.

38. Calvin, *Institutes*, chapter 15, §8.

39. Marx, K., 'Eleventh Thesis on Feuerbach', from *The German Ideology*, Lawrence and Wishart, London, 1974, p. 123.

7 Hegel's Approach to Euclid's Theory of Parallels

WOLFGANG NEUSER

Among Hegel's manuscripts of the Frankfurt period (1797-1799) is a voluminous manuscript about Euclid's geometry, which was published by J. Hoffmeister.[1] We shall attempt to examine how Hegel understands mathematical 'construction' and 'proof' in these manuscripts. The first paragraphs contain a report and interpretation of Lorenz's translation[2] of Euclid's Elements and also represents an independent reconstruction of Euclid's arguments. After treating the first twelve propositions Hegel discontinues his report and begins to reflect under which conditions something can be considered 'determined'. The last paragraph of Hegel's manuscript is clearly characterized as an insertion. He considers the limitations in space, the conditions for a proof of three-dimensionality in space and the possibilities of constructing a triangle. At the end of the paragraph Hegel returns to Euclid and incorporates propositions 27 to 31, in which the prerequisites of parallelism are implicated.[3] He ends with an exploration of conditions that must be fulfilled in order to prove the existence of parallel lines. This is the crucial point of this paper: (i) Hegel took up a fundamental and at that time pressing problem: the proof for Euclid's axioms of parallels; and (ii) Hegel reflects on the character of a 'proof', which is eminent for the structure of his later dialectical method.

I

As is well known, Euclid's book of geometry begins with **'descriptions'** defining what subsequently is to be understood under 'point', 'plane', etc.; with **'postulates'** demanding the possibility of straight lines, their steadiness and the possibility for the existence of circles everywhere in space; and with the **'axioms'** containing the 'conditions of the possibility' (Lambert) of propositions, which Euclid thereafter deduces. It had already occurred to Proklos[4] that the eleventh axiom was the only one to include an 'if-then' relationship and therefore should be deducible.[5] Therefore, until the eleventh axiom had been proved, all of Euclid's propositions not resting upon this axiom were considered proved. Up until the twenty-fifth proposition of the first book Euclid made no use of the aforementioned axiom. Hegel's own deliberations in the fragment under study begin exactly at that point at which scholars have taken a sceptical view of Euclid's argumentative force.

We know since K.F. Gauß, N. Lobachevsky, and J. Bolyai, that the axiom of parallels cannot be proved because it is a postulate: the metric of the space observed - and therewith the type of geometry on this space - have already been determined. There have been countless attempts to prove this axiom of parallels all of which either did not result in a proof or which treated the axiom as a premiss.[6]

Even J.H. Lambert made efforts to provide such a proof which, however, remained unpublished during his lifetime, as his proof was cyclical. J. Bernoulli published them in 1786.[7] What is especially interesting is that Lambert attempted to draw a distinction between the two later developed non-Euclidian geometries and the Euclidian geometry.

Lambert goes on to suppose a quadrangle in which three angles are assumed to be $90°$ angles. The remaining angle - being exactly $90°$, more than $90°$ or less than $90°$ - determines whether one has Euclidian geometry, 'geometry on a sphere' (as Lambert maintained) or hyperbolic geometry (as we say).[8]

Hegel's manuscript shows three graphic representations, which at first glance remind one of Lambert's quadrangles.[9] Hoffmeister most likely thought for this reason that Hegel apparently offered a proof like that of Lambert.[10]

However, according to mathematics there is no proof here for the axiom of parallels. On the contrary, the axiom of parallels is presupposed. Furthermore, Hegel uses for his 'proof' only a part of these figures: half of them are superfluous for his enquiries. A parallelism between Hegel and Lambert exists in another sense: Lambert explains in his letter to Baron G.J. von Holland on 11 April 1765 his assessment of Euclid's scientific method (published 1786);[11] Hegel responds to this scientific method.[12]

How does Hegel argue in this fragment? Hegel proceeds with both of Euclid's formulations for parallelism, according to which, expressed negatively, two parallel lines never meet, or, expressed positively, two lines remain infinitely equidistant.[13] The positive formulation is the starting-point for Hegel's further argumentation: 'two equidistant lines' presuppose his notion by using it as a proof that one has defined parallelism. One needs a third line, a gauge, with which one can measure at two separate points on the same line the distance between the lines that are assumed to be parallel. These lines of measurement (*Entfernungslinien*) may not, however, be drawn arbitrarily, but they should be parallel. This can be reached (i) if two shortest possible lines of measurement are both perpendicular to the lines assumed to be parallels; one then has parallel lines of measurement attained by equal angles; (ii) if the angles between the lines of measurement and the lines assumed to be parallel are arbitrary, parallelism of the lines of measurement must follow according to Euclid's proposition of inner alternate angles. This proposition assumes again the existence of parallel lines. Hegel shows in both cases that all angles between **one** of the two parallel lines and the perpendicular lines of measurement are the same (right angles). He also shows this with regard to the respective arbitrary inner alternate angles using once again only one of the parallel lines. Hence Hegel's discussion deals not with the assumed parallels themselves but with the parallelism of the lines of measurement: Lambert's square is not needed in its entirety. Mathematically this makes no sense: a proof for the parallelism of lines, which presupposes the parallelism of subsidiary lines, does not in the least prove what 'parallelism' means, as would be required for a proof of Euclid's axiom of parallels. For the moment Hegel limits his study to the characteristics of the subsidiary lines intersecting **one** of the parallel lines. The fact that he has no interest in the geometrical proof of parallelism of the assumed parallel lines is obvious. Such a proof for parallelism is not articulated. His interest is rather to probe the philosophical characteristics of geometrical proofs. That is why Hegel goes on to show what is 'necessary in determining the lines of distance'.[14] Here, as well, after a brief discussion of inner alternate angles, his assumption of the parallelism of the lines of distance follows.[15] This above-mentioned geometrical proof could lead one to believe that Lambert's theory about axioms of parallels is in the back of Hegel's mind. However, this presumption might be deficient: Lambert continuously argues with the congruence of triangles.[16] Hegel, too, constructs a quadrangle using two congruent triangles. However, he is only interested in the construction and implications of parallelism of the lines of measurement. Thus, we cannot exclude the possibility that Hegel was thinking of Lambert's proofs, but we must in any case assume that Hegel's intentions were philosophical and not mathematical.

II

The first sentences of his manuscript clearly show in what respects Euclid's axiom of parallels interested Hegel. There Hegel writes: 'In algebra, X is determined; but its determination is not established; in geometry there is no X, everything is determined and established as such, that it becomes determined is not established'.[17]

Hegel therewith describes the method that should be called upon for algebraic proofs or geometric constructions. Whereas in algebra the argument is left open - the result must still be worked out - geometry presupposes its figures. To a certain extent these figures already exist hypothetically. The further goal of the argumentation is 'merely' to show that this figure (hypothetically presupposed) can also be deduced as a figure, which is in concurrence with its notions. In a positive sense the constructive presupposition already implies what it is attempting to show. The notion establishes (*setzt*) what is to be proved in the course of argumentation. Here Hegel is in complete agreement with Lambert, who advocates the same facts of the case in a letter to Baron von Holland: according to this letter definitions have the same methodological rank as hypotheses until the possibility of a (geometrical) notion is proved. 'If it is in itself, or by a single example clear that there are at least a few such figures shown by these definitions, the definition may at first be mentioned as mere nomenclature. The condition of its possibility should, however, follow from axioms and postulates' (Point 8).[18] The realization of the possibility occurs as a geometrical construction (Points 1-6).

In conclusion, we should like briefly to mention what role Hegel's cogitations had on his later philosophical development. In his first attempt at a methodological lecture on his philosophy during his Jena period Hegel reflects upon self-activation of the 'absolute spirit' as a unity of 'construction' and 'proof'.[19] 'It is not until the proof that the necessity of construction is shown'.[20] 'Proof' and 'construction' are like the aforementioned mathematical procedures: the **proof** is a deductive result of one or several principles and leads to a result that is sought but not in fact proved from the beginning. In the case of the **construction,** on the other hand, the result is known. The goal is to show how one comes to the figure to be constructed. This characteristic of the 'absolute spirit' containing two different types of 'counter marching' proofs, is to become in Hegel's *Science of Logic* the well-known 'certification of the specific contents [*Beglaubigung des bestimmten Inhaltes*]', which 'appears regressive to the contents [*scheint rückwärts desselben zu liegen*]' (construction). Indeed, this is to be seen as 'advancing forwards [*ist aber als Vorwärtsgehen zu betrachten*]' (proof).[21] In this manner Hegel subsequently brings in the prerequisites of the argumentation in his dialectical method during the argumentation.

The argumentation in opposite directions in construction and proof in mathematics, studied by Hegel in his Frankfurt period, later became a methodological principle of his dialectical method of argumentation. We hope our considerations can indicate in what respects the pursuit of Hegel's mathematical and scientific works could be of significance in reconstructing his philosophical development.[22]

Notes

1. *DHE*, pp. 288-300.

2. J.F. Lorenz, *Elemente des Euklid,* Halle, 1798. This edition was found in Hegel's private library.

3. At best one can assume that the first part is a preparation for his function as a tutor. The part we are interested in goes beyond a simple reproduction of Euclid.

4. D. Proklos, *In primum Euclidis elementorum commentarii,* trans. L. Schönberger, Halle, 1945.

5. The method used in numbering the postulates is not standardized. In this article we will refer to the numbering used by Lorenz.

6. G.S. Klügel, *Conatuum praecipuorum theoriam parallelarum demonstrandi recensio,* Göttingen, 1763.

7. J.H. Lambert, *Theorie der Parallellinien,* in F. Engel and P. Stäckel (eds), *Die Theorie der Parallellinien,* Leipzig, 1895.

8 K. Mainzer, *Geschichte der Geometrie,* Mannheim, Wien, Zürich, 1980.

9. K. Mainzer, op.cit., p. 121.

10. *DHE*, p. 473. There are good reasons to assume that Hegel here refers to Christian Wolff, *Elementa matheseos universae: Elementa geometriae,* Halle, 1730, §§224-276, pp. 153ff. The arguments refer to the same mathematical problems and Hegel varies Wolff's figures, Table III, 56-68.

11. J.H. Lambert, *Briefwechsel,* vol. I, pp. 28-30.

12. *DHE* considers this possibility. Cf. p. 473.

13. Euclid, *Elemente der Geometrie,* description no. 35, postulate no. 11 and proposition no. 27 and following.

14. *DHE*, p. 300.

15. *DHE*, p. 300: '*EF und GH sind parallel*'. EF and GH are subsidiary lines in the proof.

16. K. Mainzer, op. cit., pp. 122 ff.

17. *DHE*, p. 329.

18. J.H. Lambert, *Briefwechsel*, vol. I, p. 30.

19. G.W.F. Hegel, *Jenenser Logik, Metaphysik und Naturphilosophie*, ed. G. Lasson, Hamburg, 1967, pp. 181, 187.

20. Ibid., p. 175.

21. G.W.F. Hegel, *Wissenschaft der Logik*, ed. E. Moldenhauer and K.M. Michel, Frankfurt, p. 554. The analogous part of the *Encyclopaedia of the Philosophical Sciences* (*HL*, p. 377) is: 'In the advance of the idea, the beginning exhibits itself as what it is implicitly. It is seen to be mediated and derivative'. See also the parallelism in the *Logic* and the *Encyclopaedia* regarding this point: the 'analytical' and the 'synthetic' manner of the philosophical method and its correspondence to the 'analytic algebra' and the 'synthetic geometry' that correspond to 'advance' and 'regress'.

22. See D. Henrich, 'Historische Voraussetzungen von Hegels System', in D. Henrich (ed.), *Hegel im Kontext*, Frankfurt, 1971, pp. 41-72.